Unbowed

WANGARI MAATHAI

Level 4

Retold by Jane Rollason
Series Editors: Andy Hopkins and Jocelyn Potter

Pearson Education Limited
Edinburgh Gate, Harlow,
Essex CM20 2JE, England
and Associated Companies throughout the world.

ISBN: 978-1-4082-6382-2

This edition first published by Pearson Education Ltd 2012

1 3 5 7 9 10 8 6 4 2

Original copyright © Wangari Maathai, 2006
Text copyright © Pearson Education Ltd 2012
Illustrations by Finn Campbell-Notmann

Set in 11/14pt Bembo
Printed in China
SWTC/01

Published by Pearson Education Limited in association with
Penguin Books Ltd, and both companies being subsidiaries of Pearson PLC

Acknowledgements:
The publisher would like to thank the following for their kind permission
to reproduce their photographs:

Corbis: Reuters / Yves Herman 70, Sygma / William Campbell 37, 44;
Getty Images: AFP / Simon Maina 63, AFP / Tony Karumba 46, Popperfoto 17
All other images © Pearson Education

Every effort has been made to trace the copyright holders and we apologise in advance
for any unintentional omissions. We would be pleased to insert the appropriate
acknowledgement in any subsequent edition of this publication.

For a complete list of the titles available in the Penguin Readers series please go to
www.penguinreaders.com. Alternatively, write to your local Pearson Longman office
or to: Penguin Readers Marketing Department, Pearson Education,
Edinburgh Gate, Harlow, Essex CM20 2JE, England.

Contents

Introduction

We saw a group of men ahead, carrying enormous knives and possibly guns. I had never been so frightened. If they discovered us, they would kill us.

Wangari Maathai (1940–2011) led an extraordinary life. Her journey took her from a childhood in the beautiful central highlands of Kenya to environmental campaigning on the world stage. In *Unbowed*, she describes that journey honestly in her own words. Maathai believes that simple acts can lead to great change, and that every problem has a solution. This is the story of one woman whose simple, brave acts helped to bring democracy back to Kenya.

Born in Nyeri, Kenya, Maathai remembers a happy early life in beautiful countryside with thick forest and wide rivers. As she grew up, she noted the first signs of damage to communities and wildlife as forests were cleared during British rule.

Maathai did well at school at a time when many people thought that education was only for boys. Then, as independence came closer, Kenya formed a new relationship with the United States and Maathai was one of hundreds of Kenyan students who were offered a place at a university in that country. This programme was organised by future president John F. Kennedy, and became known as the Kennedy Airlift.

Back in Kenya, and after many successful years teaching and studying biology at the University of Nairobi, Maathai suddenly found herself out of work. By this time, more forests had been destroyed, and the effects on the countryside were clear. She knew she had to do something. She started to put her great energy into a campaign to help the environment –

the Green Belt Movement. The idea was simple. She and her supporters used seedlings to create 'green belts' of young trees in areas where forest had gone.

Maathai fought long campaigns to save public land, to free political prisoners and to end tribal violence. She supported the fight for democracy and peace in Kenya. She became less and less popular with the government of President Moi, facing prison and beatings on several occasions. When democracy finally returned to Kenya in 2002, Maathai was elected to Kenya's parliament in the first free elections for a quarter of a century. In 2003, she was made Assistant Minister for the Environment.

Maathai received many prizes for her work in Kenya. The greatest prize of all was the Nobel Peace Prize, which she was given in 2004 for her fight for the environment, democracy and peace. She was the first African woman to receive the prize.

Wangari Maathai was admired around the world for her brave refusal to let Africans suffer. Her friends in the international community helped many times to save her life by turning a spotlight on President Moi's dishonest government. Nelson Mandela believed that Maathai's solutions would 'bring new light to Africa'. He hoped that the world would 'support her message of hope'.

Kenya is a large country, covering nearly 600,000 square kilometres in east Africa. Today it has a population of 39.8 million. The country has been described as the 'birthplace of humanity'; some of the earliest signs of human activity have been found there.

For many centuries, different tribes farmed and kept animals on the rich earth of the Kenyan highlands and valleys. Then, in 1885, the country of Kenya was created by the British and thousands of Britons settled there. The Luo, Kikuyu, Maasai and Kalenjin were four of the tribes thrown together in this new nation.

Maathai lived through a time of great change in Kenya. She was born during British rule, when many Kenyans were forced to give up their land and work for British landowners. Then in 1963, while she was studying in the United States, Kenya won its independence from Britain. Maathai returned to a country full of hope for the future. That hope slowly disappeared, though, as Kenya lost its democracy, first under President Kenyatta and then under President Moi.

Free and fair elections did not return to Kenya until the beginning of the twenty-first century. Although tribal violence returned to Nairobi and other cities after the 2007 elections, Kenya is one of the most democratic countries on the continent of Africa.

Maathai gave years of her life to the Green Belt Movement, which she started in 1977. At first, the organisation worked with small groups of women in the countryside, giving them seedlings to plant in their communities. Then it widened its activities, and it now campaigns for human rights, good government and protection of the environment. Since it was started, Green Belt women have planted more than thirty million trees across Kenya, making a real difference to the environmental health of the country. And the trees are not just about the environment. 'The planting of trees is the planting of ideas,' says Maathai. 'By starting with the simple act of planting a tree, we give hope to ourselves and to our children.' You can find out more about the work of the organisation at www.greenbeltmovement.org.

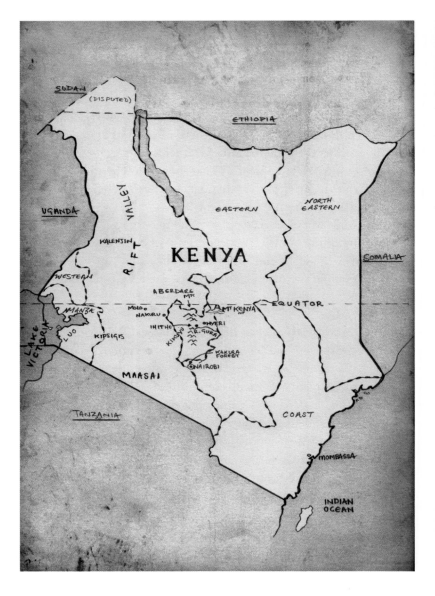

Kenya, homeland of Wangari Maathai

Chapter 1 The Fig Tree

I was born on 1 April 1940, the third of six children, in the small village of Ihithe in the central mountains of Kenya. To the north, the great Mount Kenya cut into the skyline.

My family lived in a traditional African house with mud walls, without electricity or running water. My parents were poor farmers and members of the Kikuyu tribe, the largest community in Kenya. We grew our own food, and kept cows and sheep.

In those days, the land around Ihithe was still green and the earth was rich. The seasons were always the same, with the long, heavy rains starting in the middle of March. The winter weather came in July, when it was so cold that some birds froze to death in the trees. The land was thickly covered with trees and plants. Clean drinking water was everywhere. Vegetables grew in the fields and nobody was hungry.

When a baby was born, village women brought seasonal fruit and vegetables to the new mother. She put juice from each of these into the baby's little mouth. So I tasted the fruits of the land even before my mother's milk. I am a child of the earth, as well as a child of my mother and father.

At 5,199 metres above sea level, Mount Kenya is the second highest mountain in Africa. It was a very important place for the Kikuyus in the time of my grandparents, and the doors of their houses faced the mountain. When clouds collected on top of the mountain, they were often followed by rain. While the rains fell, people felt that God was with them. They had enough food, and could live in peace. Sadly, these beliefs have now gone. They were already dying when I was born.

In 1885, when European countries were called the 'great powers', some of them met in Berlin, Germany. They had a map of Africa in front of them, and with a pen they gave control of different parts of the continent to each country. In East Africa, Germany received modern Tanzania; Britain received Kenya and Uganda. But before 1885, Kenya did not exist. The different 'nations' of Africa were the different tribes. The Maasai lived beside the Kikuyu. Sometimes they fought, but usually they traded. These new African 'countries' put together communities with different languages, different cultures and different traditions. The effects of these decisions still cause problems in Africa today.

When the Europeans came, they brought new medicines. Traditional African medicines could not cure some diseases, and the Europeans introduced treatments for these. They brought a new religion – the Christian religion. God lives in heaven, they taught the local people, not on Mount Kenya. Next, they taught adults to read and opened schools. Reading and writing seemed to the Kikuyu like a new form of magic, and they loved it. Europeans brought new farming methods too. They cut down the Kenyan trees and planted non-native trees. They hunted the wildlife and gave new European names to everything.

Many Europeans came to settle in Africa in the new countries. In Kenya, the British government gave the settlers land in the highlands. They took this land from native people, and it became known as the 'white highlands'. The land here was good, and the climate was perfect. At the same time, the British allowed some local people to keep their land in special native areas. The Kikuyu area included our village of Ihithe, where my father owned land.

Not all Kenyans became Christians, but Christian Kenyans were more likely to get jobs in the British government. People believed that Christian Kenyans were modern – they were moving forwards into tomorrow's world. If a Kikuyu wanted to keep Kikuyu customs, people thought that he or she was living in the past. By the time of my birth, Kikuyus had begun to forget their own culture. They drank tea and cooked in iron pots. They ate with spoons instead of with their fingers and sticks. The women wore cotton dresses instead of animal skins. The men wore shirts and trousers. Women grew their hair long. Men cut their hair short. They sang new songs and they learned new dances.

My parents had also become Christians, and dressed like Europeans. My father was tall and strong. Some older people still remember his strength: 'Your father was so strong, he didn't need any tools to change the wheel of his car.' Nobody ever started a fight with my father, because he never lost.

My mother was tall and thin. Although she did not look strong, she had a strong character and was very hardworking. She was gentle and kind, and never shouted. Girls did not go to school when my mother was young, so she never learned to read or write. All her life was spent in the fields, and she was still growing her own vegetables in her eighties. I was her eldest daughter and we were very close. When you are the first girl in a Kikuyu family, you become the second woman in the house. You are your mother's right hand and you are always with her.

When my father was a young man, many Kikuyu men had to leave their families and native areas, and take jobs on white farms. In 1943, my mother and I joined my father. He had found a job as a driver and mechanic on a farm in Nakuru, in the Rift Valley, about 150 kilometres away. The British farm owner, Mr Neylan, valued my father for his skills and hardworking attitude. Although he earned little, my father was given land to build a house and grow food for his family. The land was good and we were never hungry.

My mother had two more daughters after we moved to

Nakuru. As a young child, I went into the fields with my mother to help look after my sisters. She put us on the ground near her, and we played while she worked. We had our jobs too. We took our sheep to eat grass. It was very pleasant. Wonderful *managu* fruits grew wild in the fields, and we ate them all day. You do not see *managu* today – modern farming methods have destroyed the plant.

In those days, Kikuyu men often had several wives, and my father had four. We all lived in one compound; several houses were surrounded by a fence with a gate. My father lived in a *thingira*, a large round hut made of mud and wood, with a grass roof. He ate, slept and received guests there. I sometimes took food to him from my mother, but I did not stay – this hut was a man's world. Each wife had a *nyũmba*, a house with different areas in one room. There were three sleeping places – one for my mother, one for her daughters and one for my older brothers.

As in Ihithe, the houses had no electricity or running water. There were small windows, but they had no glass. In the middle of the *nyũmba* was a fire. My mother prepared meals over the fire, and here we talked and told stories. The mud walls were kept warm by the heat from the fire, so it was never cold, even in winter.

We were a community. Everyone in the compound was a member of our family. I could go to any of the other wives' houses and feel at home. I called other wives 'younger mother' or 'older mother'. My own mother was just 'mother'.

In traditional Kikuyu society, a father took care of all his children. If he did not, the villagers threw him out or stopped speaking to him. In those days, that mattered. Today, it does not seem to matter. I have learned since then that there were problems between the wives, and that my father beat them. As a child, I did not see any of that.

Groups of Kikuyus, Luos and Kipsigis all worked on Mr Neylan's farm. Each community did a different kind of work – Kikuyus worked in the fields, Luos worked in the house and Kipsigis looked after the animals. The communities did not mix. We did not speak each other's languages or share cultures – the Luos were as foreign to me as the British.

During my years on the farm, I never thought about skin colour. I saw the difference in lifestyle, but I just accepted it. I never spoke to the Neylans, but I know they were good people. I loved watching Mrs Neylan. She always wore a large hat because of the strong African sun. She wore flowery cotton dresses and people called her *nyakĩneke*, which means 'a large person'. I often saw Mrs Neylan when I went to the main house to fetch my family's milk. She was usually collecting eggs from her chickens. If she saw me today, she would probably say, 'Look at you! Who is *nyakĩneke* now!'

Although my father and Mr Neylan were never equals, they became good friends. When, in 1963, Kenya won its independence from Britain, many British farmers sold their land to local people. But Mr Neylan decided to give my father a piece of land, and my father and others were able to buy the rest of the farm. My father loved that land. My oldest brother lives there now.

As a child on Mr Neylan's farm, I occasionally went with my mother to the town of Nakuru, about sixteen kilometres away. There were no buses in those days, so we walked, arriving in Nakuru at daybreak. We knew we were close when we saw the jacaranda trees, with their blue-purple flowers. A visit to town was a great adventure for a country girl. I could not believe the cars, people, clothes and things for sale. We drank tea at a hotel.

5

Like many towns in British Kenya, Nakuru had separate areas for Europeans, Indians and Africans. The Europeans lived on the hill above the town in red brick houses. The Indians lived halfway up the hill in houses with flat roofs and small gardens. The British had brought Indians to Kenya in the 1890s to build the railway. Many stayed and opened shops, introducing new foods, like salt, fat, sugar and oil. These were unknown to Africans and tasted very good, but today many common diseases in Africa are the result of this sudden change in everyday food; until then, Kikuyus had eaten mainly maize, beans and green vegetables. The Africans lived in the most crowded part of town. The stone, mud or brick homes were small and close together. I could see the difference, even as a child. But I did not think the races were separated intentionally. We belonged in that part of town.

Today the jacarandas are still there, but Nakuru is not as beautiful as it was. Many Europeans and Indians have stayed, but the communities are mixed. Now, money talks. If you have it, you can live anywhere.

In 1947, I moved with my mother and sisters back to my parents' village of Ihithe. My two older brothers were already there, living with my uncle. They were attending school in Nyeri, because there were no schools near Mr Neylan's farm.

My grandfather received us warmly. He seemed very old to me. He wore a blanket around his shoulders and colourful earrings in his long ears.

The people of Ihithe were farmers. There were no European farms there, so everyone lived and worked in one place. It rained often, but the rivers were always clean because plants grew thickly along the banks. The adults told us to play in the rain. 'You will get tall, like the maize,' they said. I loved it. In some ways, Ihithe has not changed much today. There is a hairdresser's, a medical centre and a café, but sheep are still eating grass by the road. The men have still not finished the conversation that they began a thousand years ago. The women are still selling their vegetables or carrying firewood on their backs. Children are still walking to school, although now the schools are built of stone, not mud.

Soon after our return to Ihithe, my uncle built a house for us. It was a mud hut with two rooms, one for sleeping and one for cooking and sitting in. My older brothers lived in a small hut behind the main house. I collected firewood every day. I loved to carry the wood on my back and sing as I walked home, just like my mother. I washed my older brothers' clothes and took food to them, as was expected. I went to the fields with my mother.

A few months after we arrived, my mother suddenly felt unwell. She sent me to fetch her grandmother, Wangui. Soon, my mother had had a new baby. My brother Kamunya was her last child. I had not even known that my mother was expecting a baby.

My mother gave me my own small garden. She showed me how to plant and look after vegetables. I planted sweet potatoes, beans and maize. Sometimes I lifted the seeds out of the ground to see if they were growing. 'No, no!' my mother said. 'Don't touch them. Soon they will come above the ground.' When they did, I was very surprised.

At about this time, something serious started to happen in the forests. We saw enormous fires as the natural forests went up in smoke. The British government had decided to plant non-native trees, like pine, eucalyptus and black wattle. These trees grew fast and strongly; their wood was used for building, and was sold abroad. Local farmers were given seedlings of these new trees. They planted them because the trees grew so fast and could be sold.

But these trees did damage too. They killed local plants and

Trees of Kenya

animals, destroying the natural life of the forest. When rains fell, much of the water ran to lower ground because there were no plants to hold it back. Underground water levels began to fall, and eventually some rivers became dry.

♦

'Why doesn't Wangari go to school like the rest of us?' asked one of my older brothers one day.

My mother thought for a moment. This was a big decision. She had had no education herself. She had three young children to look after. Then there was the cost.

'There's no reason why not,' she said.

I was eight years old and that decision changed my life.

Ihithe School had mud walls, an earth floor and a tin roof. The teachers looked after the children well, but they were also very strict. They beat children who disobeyed them. There were adults in our class as well as children. These older students complained when the teachers told them to sweep the floor or fetch water.

Over the next three years, I learned Kiswahili and English, Kenya's two official languages, and maths. The teachers were serious, responsible and kind, and I was a good student. At the end of my time at Ihithe School, I got very good marks in the national exam, so I was able to continue my education.

I loved learning, but I also loved nature. There were great forests around Ihithe, full of wildlife. People often saw leopards, the most feared animals in the area. The Kikuyu word for leopard is *ngarĩ*, and *wa-ngarĩ*, like my name, means 'of the leopard'. 'Leopards hide among thick plants in the forest,' my mother explained, 'and hang their tails across narrow paths. Do not step on a leopard's tail. Tell it, "You and I are both leopards, so you have no reason to hurt me."'

There were wild fig trees all over the country. Thick plants grew underneath fig trees and the birds loved their fruits. A very large fig tree grew near our house. When I went to collect firewood, my mother said, 'Remember not to pick any dry wood from the fig tree. It's a tree of God. We don't use it. We don't cut it. We don't burn it.'

A beautiful stream ran past the fig tree. The water was clean and fresh. As a child, I loved to play there. But I later learned that the stream was there because of the fig tree. The roots of the fig went deep into the ground, breaking through the rocks into underground lakes. The water travelled along the roots and then pushed through the ground, making a stream. The local people did not realise it, but their cultural practice was an important part of the life of the natural world.

Many evenings, at the end of a day in the fields, we sat around an open fire. While the meal was cooking, the children listened to the women telling stories. Sometimes we were frightened and sometimes we laughed, but we were always entertained. And as the women told the stories, they shared with us the knowledge and values of our Kikuyu community.

Our experiences as children stay with us when we become adults. Although I was entering a world of books and facts, I still enjoyed a world with no books, with living stories. In this world we were close to the earth and our imaginations grew like the seeds that we planted in the ground.

Chapter 2 A Leopard in the Moonlight

Have you ever woken up and the day looks ordinary, and then something extraordinary happens that changes your life for ever? It was a day like that when I discovered my mother, my brother Nderitu and my cousin Wangari Wanguku deep in conversation about me. Before I could hear anything interesting, my mother saw me and sent me to fetch water.

I raced back as fast as I could, trying not to drop the water. But the conversation had ended and they had already made their decision. I was going to join my cousin at St Cecilia's School, a Catholic school on Nyeri hill. The school was run by Italian nuns.

My emotions at that moment were very mixed. I was happy because I was going to St Cecilia's and I knew it was a good school. I was sad because I was leaving my mother and I was only eleven years old. It was a day's walk to the school, and I would live there in term time. And I was sad too because I was leaving my family and friends, our animals and gardens, and the small stream that I visited every day.

I later learned that my family had one worry about St Cecilia's. They were afraid that I would become a nun and join the religious community for ever. Kikuyu people expected girls to marry and have children. They did not want me to give my life to God.

My mother gave me a small wooden box and I packed my few things. She cut my hair very short, so it was easy to look after, and bought me a new dress. My brother bought me one too. He had bought some green material for some trousers for himself, and he bought extra so that I could have a dress. I was very pleased.

The great day came. I carried my box on my back in the same way that I carried firewood. My family walked with me until I met my cousin Wangari at the top of the hill outside our village. I said goodbye and began my new life.

The journey took a day. We had to cross a wide, fast river on a narrow footbridge. Below me the river was black and angry, and I was worried that I would fall in. Wangari told me to look ahead and walk straight across. Later, we came over the top of a hill, and there in the next valley we saw the school. It was built in an Italian style, with stone buildings and red roofs. The land was owned by the Catholic Church as far as we could see.

We arrived at bedtime. Wangari joined her class, and I went to the room for first-year students. Thirty of us slept in one big room. It was quite an experience. I had a bed with sheets and pillows. The bed was filled with grass, and it made a noise every time I moved. But to me, it was a bed fit for a queen. One of the nuns came into the room. She wore long white clothes and a black cross around her neck.

The next morning, a bell woke us. We washed and tidied our beds, and then dressed. We went to church for an hour and had maize for breakfast. After breakfast we cleaned. We cut the grass, swept the paths, cleaned the bathrooms and tidied the bedrooms. Finally, we went to class, where we studied all day with a break for lunch. The evening meal was at five. The food was the same every day: beans for lunch, *ugali* (a dish of maize cooked with water) and vegetables for dinner. We had no snacks, so when we got to the dining room we were very hungry. Everyone ate what was placed in front of them, although there were often little insects in the maize and the beans. There was an hour of homework after dinner, and then it was bedtime. We did not wear shoes because most of us did not have any, so we always washed our feet at night. Then we went to bed, laughing and talking on the way. And that was my day, every day, for four years.

I really enjoyed learning. I was a careful listener and paid attention in class, although I was very playful outside it. I was never bored at St Cecilia's because I kept very busy. There was never time to lie in the sun and do nothing. That was a pity – I know that now. It is good, especially for a young person, to enjoy the sun and watch the clouds in the sky.

Although the school had electricity and running water, life was hard. The mud walls of our house in Ihithe kept the heat in, but the stone walls of St Cecilia's let the cold in. There was no heating or hot water in the bedrooms. During the cool seasons, when you washed your face in the morning, the icy water certainly woke you up.

Our families could visit one day a month. Sometimes my brother Nderitu came more often, but I was not allowed to see him. I knew that he came because he was interested in my progress. The cost of St Cecilia's was hard for my family, and although Nderitu was then still at Kagumo High School, he did small jobs to help pay for my education. For example, he boiled water on a small heater in his room for other students for a few coins.

At first I missed my family, but I soon made some very good friends – friends that I still have today. The nuns were kind, and tried to be mothers to us. Sister Germana, from Milan in northern Italy, was very loving. Although she was young and beautiful, she had given herself to God and had come to serve strangers in a quiet corner of the world.

There were punishments, though. The worst crime was not speaking English. By this time, English had become the official language in Kenyan schools. You could not progress with your studies if you spoke bad English. Many schools told their students to speak English at all times, even during the holidays. If a teacher heard you speaking Kikuyu, she punished you. At the end of the day, you had to cut the grass, sweep the paths or work in the garden. The work was easy; the feeling of embarrassment in front of your friends was hard. So we all spoke English from morning until night. This practice continues in some Kenyan schools today, but it has a bad effect on African children. It makes African culture and language seem less important than Western culture. It makes children doubt themselves. In fact, language is very important for communication but also to carry culture, knowledge and history. I am very glad I did not forget how to speak Kikuyu; some of our educated children cannot connect with their parents, but this did not happen to me.

St Cecilia's changed us in other ways too. Kikuyu dancing, singing and story-telling disappeared from our lives. Now we read books, studied and played Western sports. I also belonged to a Christian group that taught us to help our community. We visited hospitals and helped the nurses. We worked in the school gardens and helped other students with homework. We were asked to serve God by serving other people.

During my time at St Cecilia's, I decided to become a Catholic, and I took new Christian names: Mary Josephine. My friends called me Mary Jo through high school and college.

♦

In 1952, towards the end of my first year at St Cecilia's, there was trouble in Kenya. During the Second World War, many Kenyan men fought for the British in Somalia, Ceylon (now Sri Lanka) and Burma (now Myanmar). When these soldiers returned after the war, in 1945, they were given nothing for their service; their bravery was not recognised. In fact, the British government took away some of their land and gave it to British soldiers. These Kenyan soldiers were from the Kikuyu, Meru and Embu tribes, and their anger became a rebellion against British rule – it was called the Mau Mau rebellion.

Kikuyus had a much older complaint against the British, and this was the root of the Mau Mau anger. In 1890, a British captain called Frederick Lugard had arranged a meeting with a Kikuyu leader, Waiyaki. Captain Lugard wanted to build British trading stations on Kikuyu land, but he promised not to take Kikuyu land or other property. Waiyaki agreed and the two men shook hands. The agreement did not last long. Lugard's men immediately took

Kikuyu property and attacked Kikuyu women. A war started between the British and the Kikuyus, ending in 1892, when Waiyaki was caught. Lugard's men put him in a hole in the ground. Before he was dead, they filled the hole with earth.

In Kikuyu culture, everybody has a right to a home and space. People with land were expected to share with people who had no land. The behaviour of Lugard and the British was deeply shocking. But the British were not interested in the feelings of the native population, and continued to take Kikuyu land.

In the early years of the twentieth century, all the peoples of Kenya rebelled against foreign rule. Many people were killed and eventually the British won. After the First World War, the British introduced a new law: every male African in Kenya had to carry a document with personal details on it. They forced Kenyans to work for them and they increased taxes. Local men began to organise to fight for better conditions, but the British used violence to stop them. In 1922, African organisations and newspapers were closed down.

All this bad feeling fed the desire for independence. During the Second World War, many of the Kenyan soldiers had learned new fighting skills in the forests of Burma. Their war experience had also opened their eyes to the political situation in Kenya, and they began to organise a campaign for independence. One of the organisers of this campaigning group, the Kenyan African Union (KAU), was called Jomo Kenyatta.

But change was slow and some Kenyans lost patience. In the early 1950s, when I was studying at St Cecilia's, Kenyans used their experience of war to fight the British. The Mau Mau began a war for independence. They had three aims: land, freedom and independence for Kenyans.

At St Cecilia's, we were protected from the violence most of the time. We believed what the British told us: the Mau Maus

15

were a terror group and wanted to take Kenya back to the nineteenth century. I did not understand that the Mau Maus were our freedom fighters!

Through the 1950s, we often saw soldiers on both sides of the rebellion in and around Nyeri. As well as the Mau Mau fighters, there were 50,000 British soldiers in Kenya, helped by the Home Guards. The Home Guards were Kikuyus who fought for the British against the Mau Maus. All healthy males had to belong to the Home Guard, watching for attacks at night. My older brothers helped them during the holidays.

It was not a safe time for young girls. One night, during the holidays, I was staying with my cousin Wangari in our village of Ihithe with two other girls and a small baby. We heard gunshots near the house, and Wangari's mother took us to hide among a group of black wattle trees. The trees were thick and dark and that night the moon was very bright. We put the baby on the ground to continue sleeping. Suddenly, our hearts began to beat very fast. Perhaps seven metres away, a leopard passed us in the moonlight. Would the baby wake up and start to cry? But the leopard did not even look at us, and disappeared through the trees. We looked at each other and smiled. Our hearts calmed down a little.

The Mau Mau rebellion created terror among the white settlers, and many Kikuyu supporters were put in prison camps. The British built 'villages' for women, children and the old, where hunger and disease were common. My mother was forced to live in one of these. She and my father did not see each other for seven years at this time. In 1953, Kenyatta was sent to a camp for seven years, and a year later, ten thousand Mau Mau fighters were put in camps. Land was taken from the prisoners and given to Home Guards who had been loyal to the British.

I was arrested only once during the rebellion, when I was seventeen. It was during the school holidays, and I was on my

There were 50,000 British soldiers in Kenya,
helped by the Home Guards.

way to visit my family in Nakuru. I was allowed to travel, but when I reached Nakuru I was arrested. I had the correct document, but it showed that I was from Nyeri. I was a long way from home, so perhaps that was why. I was a Kikuyu in the wrong place at the wrong time.

I was very frightened. The conditions were horrible. There were no toilets, there was very little food, and the camp was very crowded. I found a space to sleep. Because I was wearing school uniform, people asked me why I was in the camp. There was a strange calmness there. Children were not crying, and I made sure that I did not cry. Men and women spoke kindly to me, and they were worried about me. I was questioned, and after two long days the police took me to my father. They probably called Mr Neylan and he told them to let me go.

The true cost of the British response to the Mau Mau rebellion has recently been studied. Four thousand people died as a result of Mau Mau activity; of these, only thirty-two were white settlers. In comparison, it is thought that more than one hundred thousand Africans, mostly Kikuyus, lost their lives in the camps. Nothing has been done to help people free themselves from the memories of this terrible time, and the resulting damage is still affecting these families today.

◆

I was top of the class in my final exams at St Cecilia's. I left in 1956, and went to Loreto Girls' High School in Nairobi. This was a Catholic school run by Irish nuns, and students attended from all over Kenya. For the first time, I was studying with girls from different tribes and areas.

I had a very good science teacher there. During breaks, she asked me to help her with her work. Through our many conversations, she planted the seeds of my interest in science.

The Loreto nuns also ran an all-white girls' school near

ours. At that time, I did not find it strange. Nobody discussed it. My classmates and I did not see this as discrimination. The world was organised that way.

I learned from the nuns and from Kikuyu culture to look for the best in people and in society. I believe a positive attitude towards life and other human beings is healthy for a person, and helps to bring change.

Although my education gave me a way out of a hard life in the fields, I have always been connected to the earth. And although I only saw my mother during the holidays, we stayed close. I put away my education when I went home, and helped my mother. I repaired the mud walls of her house when they needed it. My work looked good, and my mother was happy.

Towards the end of my time at Loreto High School, my friends and I had to think about the future. Many of my classmates expected to be teachers or nurses because there were not many other opportunities for women in 1959.

'I don't want to be a teacher or a nurse,' I said. 'I'm going to go to Makerere University.'

Makerere was in Uganda, and at that time it was the only university in East Africa. But it was hard to get a place there.

'What will you do if you don't pass?' my teachers and friends asked.

'Of course I will pass!' I replied.

But then an opportunity beyond my dreams arrived – an opportunity to study in the United States.

Chapter 3 American Dream

By the time I left high school in 1959, change was coming to Africa. Many countries were winning independence from their European rulers. Freedom was in the air in Kenya too.

In 1957, black Kenyans won the vote for the first time, and in 1959 the British government invited Kenyan politicians to London to discuss a new Kenyan government. The following year, preparations began for Kenya's independence.

The new independent Kenya would need educated men and women to fill important posts in government and society. Contact was made with political and cultural figures in the United States, including future president John F. Kennedy. Good students from African states were offered places at American universities. In return, African nations would begin to trade with the United States. Until now, European rulers had kept African economies closed to the rest of the world. Under Kennedy's plan, called the Kennedy Airlift, nearly six hundred Kenyans were flown to different colleges and universities in the United States.

I had just completed my education at Loreto High School at the top of the class. I was in the right place at the right time. When I was offered the opportunity to study in the United States, I did not need time to think.

'Yes!' I said.

I was very excited about this great opportunity. My parents were very happy too. It was very surprising news in my village, where many people still did not believe in girls' education.

In September 1960, a whole new world opened to me. You can imagine my feelings as I boarded a plane for the first time. I was twenty years old, and a life of new experiences was ahead of me. The plane flew over the Sahara Desert and I could not believe it. You can read about the size of the Sahara in school books, but you cannot really understand its size until you see with your own eyes. The journey took days, with stops in Libya, Luxembourg, Iceland and Newfoundland, before we finally arrived in New York City.

Had we landed on the moon? It felt like it. I was with a

friend, Agatha Wangeci, and together we tried to understand this strange city. We stared up at the tall buildings, which seemed to touch the clouds. We went in lifts. I had once been in a lift in Nairobi – to the fourth floor. In New York we went up in lifts at lightning speed to the twentieth and thirtieth floors. I was very pleased to reach the ground floor again and get out.

I was very surprised by the number of black Americans in New York. These Americans were as dark as me but did not speak English with Kenyan accents. I had expected black Americans to be light-skinned.

I knew so little about the United States. In those days in Kenya, there were few radios, no television, few films and no pop music, and American culture had not reached the villages. I did not even know that Coca-Cola was an American drink.

We did not stay long in New York City. A special bus was taking the African students to their different destinations in the Mid-West. Agatha and I were going to Atchison, Kansas – the last stop. The journey took more than two days. At each stop, a few more students left the bus until there were ten of us left. At one stop, we decided to get a drink at a local café. The girls looked around for a place to sit while the boys went up to the counter to order. But a few moments later, they returned.

'We can't sit down and have a drink,' they told us.

'Why not?' we asked.

'Because we're black,' they replied.

The café owner said we could have a drink outside.

'Why should we drink outside?' we said. We could not believe it. So we left and got back on the bus. That was my first experience of racial discrimination in the United States, and I was shocked.

We had studied very little of African American history at school in Kenya. We knew that Africans were taken across the

21

Atlantic and sold, but we had not learned about the terrible treatment they received. We Africans have to go to the United States to understand the history of our own people.

The bus finally arrived in Atchison, a small town beside the Missouri River. The women's college was called Mount St Scholastica, and the students called themselves 'Mounties'. Like all my earlier schools, the college was run by Catholic nuns. Agatha and I received a wonderful, warm welcome that continued for the whole of our stay. I never felt lonely or homesick.

We arrived in the middle of the campaign for the 1960 presidential election. John F. Kennedy and Richard Nixon were fighting to be president. We knew nothing about American politics, but naturally we were Kennedy supporters. He had made possible our stay in the United States. He was a Catholic too, which added to the excitement. Local Kennedy supporters asked us to speak about their leader at a campaign meeting. It was a great introduction to college culture. We had not even unpacked our cases, and we were already part of the presidential campaign. We celebrated with everyone else when Kennedy won.

The education at the Mount was less strict than at high school in Kenya; we questioned ideas and facts much more. I continued to specialise in science, but added German to my studies. Classes were difficult at first; although Agatha and I spoke English as our second language, we found native speakers difficult to understand.

I was very surprised at the freedom enjoyed by students. Young men and women kissed in public. They held hands in front of the nuns, who said nothing. We were allowed to watch romantic films. And at the weekends, students had parties for men and women, who danced *with each other*.

This freedom was wonderful, but also worrying. It went against the teaching of the nuns in Kenya. 'Why was dancing so wrong?' I began to think. 'Is it so bad if a girl holds a boy's hand?' I realised that my earlier education was very out of date. I had lived like a nun myself.

♦

Kansas was very different from the central highlands, which are full of valleys and mountains. Atchison is completely flat. I enjoyed long walks along the Missouri River, and experiencing the big changes from season to season. We arrived in autumn, when the leaves on the trees were green, yellow, gold, red and brown. And then they all fell off the trees, leaving them looking dead. Of course leaves fall from trees in Kenya, but never all at the same time and in such enormous quantities.

And then there was the snow! I had seen the white ice on top of Mount Kenya, but I had never seen snow fall. The really freezing weather came in January. I had never been as cold as I was during those winter months. Winter in Atchison had a special sound too. As the wind blew through the leafless trees, it whispered. At first it seemed strange and frightening, but I learned to love that sound. It reminded me of romantic music.

Spring was also new to my senses. I loved to watch young green leaves suddenly appear on the trees after the snow had gone.

Summer in Kansas was too hot. Agatha and I complained about the heat. The Americans could not understand it.

'We thought you'd enjoy this weather,' they said.

But we were dreaming of the cold highland air of the Kenyan mountains.

It was not possible to go home for a visit. The journey was too long and expensive. We knew that when we went home, it would be at the end of our studies. Even our letters often took six months to arrive. Luckily, I made some good friends at the Mount. One friend, Florence Conrad, was like a sister to me. She took me to her family home near Wichita for Christmas, Thanksgiving and Easter. I felt completely at home with

Florence, her many brothers and sisters and her loving parents. We spent evenings talking at the kitchen table, drinking coffee and eating Christmas cookies.

If I stayed at college during the holidays, I helped the nuns in the kitchen, or I packed books with my great friend Sister Gonzaga to send to her favourite schools in the Philippines.

There was a good international community at the Mount, and I had friends from China, India and Japan. Sometimes the local press interviewed us, or we were asked to speak about our countries to local schools. We organised an international night at college, when we shared our cultures with our friends. One time, I dressed as a Kikuyu girl, with a sheet over my shoulder, and taught my friends some Kikuyu dances.

Agatha and I occasionally went dancing with the Kenyan boys from the men's college in Atchison. In our first year, we were still learning to dance to American music. Some of the boys had been in the United States for several years and they criticised us. They told us to be more like American girls, and to straighten our hair with a hot comb. We were not in a hurry to become Kenyan Americans, but by our third year, we were first on the dance floor with all the latest moves. We even used the hot comb on our hair.

The only time I personally experienced racial discrimination in the United States was on that first bus journey. But I saw it on television. Many white Americans hated blacks, and there were marches in the streets. We often saw the police beating African Americans. I think I was lucky. Kenyan students in other towns and cities experienced discrimination when they looked for jobs and places to stay, or when they tried to make friends.

Then on 22 November 1963, we had a terrible shock. President Kennedy was shot dead in Dallas, Texas. When the news reached us, the college closed and the students were sent home. Agatha and I stayed at the college, following events on television. The shooting was shown again and again. And as we watched, the killer, Lee Harvey Oswald, was murdered too. 'I admired President Kennedy as a leader and a lover of peace,' I wrote to my brother Nderitu. I had been part of his dream, coming to the United States from Africa. It felt like a member of my family had died.

A few weeks later, we had something to celebrate. We did not get much news from Kenya, but we learned that on 12 December 1963, Kenya had finally won independence from Britain. All the Kenyans in Kansas travelled to the city of Lawrence. We sang, danced and listened to speeches, as Jomo Kenyatta became Kenya's first African leader.

◆

I learned a lot during my four years at the Mount, as well as completing my degree. Now I was even more willing to listen and learn, to think carefully about things and to ask questions.

I wanted to continue my studies, and I won a place at the University of Pittsburgh in Pennsylvania to take a Master's* degree in biology. There, guided by Professor Charles Ralph, I studied the brains of small birds and improved my scientific skills. These skills were very useful later, in Kenya.

There were a lot of factories in Pittsburgh, and by the mid-1960s the air was very dirty. Nobody hung their washing out to dry because it turned black. People had to paint their houses every year because they looked as dirty as the inside of a chimney. The city wanted to change, so it began an environmental campaign to clean the air. This was my first experience of a 'green' campaign. Over the years it has been successful, and people in Pittsburgh can now hang out their washing.

* Master's, PhD: higher university degrees. A Master's degree usually takes one year of study after a first degree. A PhD takes three years or more.

As I completed my studies in Pittsburgh, Kenya was celebrating two years of independence. British officials were leaving their posts in Nairobi, and the Kenyan government sent people to the United States to employ young Kenyans and bring them back. I was interviewed by someone from the University of Nairobi. A professor there was running a programme to control desert insects, and he needed an assistant. These insects ate anything green, and were a real problem. I got the job and was told to report for work on 10 January 1966. I even received a handwritten letter from the professor, with details of the job offer. This was my first 'real' job.

♦

I returned to Kenya with a belief in working hard and helping the poor and the weak. I wanted to teach in a university and share my knowledge. I wanted to see my family and start my own family. And I had a new name. I had dropped my Catholic name and was now Wangari Muta. I was proud of being African, and I wanted to show that in my name.

The United States gave me confidence as an African woman, and made me the person I am today. It taught me not to waste any opportunity. I had found a sense of freedom and possibility in the United States, and I wanted Kenyans to share that feeling.

Chapter 4 A Good African Woman

Five and a half years after leaving Kenya, I was back. I stepped off the plane into the warm, dry air and saw my family and friends waving madly at me. Tears ran down my face as I ran into the airport building. I had not expected anyone to meet me in Nairobi. They had travelled a long way to welcome me home. When I finally got through passport control, there were kisses, handshakes, questions and more tears. We had all changed. We were greyer, taller or thinner.

'Nderitu!' I cried to my oldest brother.

'No,' he laughed, 'I am Kamunya.'

'Kamunya,' I replied, embarrassed, to my younger brother. 'You've grown so tall!'

'And you,' said my parents. 'What happened? You're so thin! Didn't you eat enough?'

In the United States, people thought I was just right: thin, but not too thin. I was the perfect size for the tight dress I was wearing that day.

We all squeezed into an old car lent by a friend. As we drove through Nairobi, I sensed a great excitement about the future of Kenya. President Kenyatta was speaking on the car radio. We must go back to the countryside, he was saying, we must grow tea and coffee, we must build a strong economy. As we listened, we all felt proud and ready to help with the building of our free country.

After a few days, my family returned to the countryside and I prepared to report for work. On that Monday, I went to the science department at the University of Nairobi with my letter from the professor. I knocked on the professor's door and introduced myself enthusiastically.

'Oh,' he said. 'The job has been offered to someone else.'

I was shocked. I held up the letter.

'But you wrote me this letter,' I said. It was on official university paper and he had signed it himself. 'I've come all the way from the United States.'

He was not interested. I went to his boss and explained my situation. He supported the professor.

'Because the letter is handwritten,' he said, 'it is not official.'

I went from office to office. I discovered that the job really had gone to someone else, a man from the professor's own tribe. And that man was still in Canada. Was it because I was a woman or because I was a Kikuyu? There was nothing I could do.

It was not easy to find another job. One day when I was job-hunting, I met a relative called Nderitu Mathenge, who worked at the new School of Animal Medicine at the University of Nairobi. He invited me to stay with his family in Nairobi. Nderitu and Elizabeth, his wife, were very kind and protective.

'Don't worry,' they said. 'You'll get a job.'

In their house I met Reinhold Hofmann, a German professor who was working in the same School as Nderitu. By chance, Professor Hofmann was looking for an assistant. He interviewed me and offered me the job for two reasons. First, I had learned many scientific skills while taking my biology degree at the University of Pittsburgh. These skills were exactly what he was looking for. And second, I spoke German. A lot of Germans worked in Professor Hofmann's department and many of the coursebooks were in German too. In the years that followed, the university became my second home as I lost myself in books and biology. I progressed in the department and eventually became a member of the teaching team, and I began to study for a PhD.

I loved working with the students as they began their university lives. They were young and enthusiastic. When I started teaching, all the students were male. I was a woman in my mid-twenties. How could I teach them biology? My male colleagues were often difficult too. 'Do you really have a Master's degree?' they asked, laughing. I knew they doubted my ability. I also knew that I knew more than they did. The students quickly learned who was boss. A bad mark from me was the same as one from my male colleagues. That was a language they understood.

I received a university flat, near the female students'

housing. It was very safe and close to town. I also bought myself a car, although I did not know how to drive. It gave me a great feeling of independence. My life was perfect.

♦

Nairobi in the 1960s was known as the Green City in the Sun. It was a pleasant place to live, with many open spaces. Fewer than half a million people lived there, a sixth of its population today. There were no street children and no areas of poor housing. The buses were never crowded, rubbish was collected and the whole city was clean. My women friends and I often walked among the small shops and cafés in the city centre without fear.

Nairobi nightlife was good too. We went out to clubs and danced to British and American music. While we were enjoying ourselves, many of our friends were getting married.

'This freedom won't last for ever,' they told us.

My family did not tell me to look for a husband, but my aunt often talked about the importance of marriage when I was in Ihithe, and looked at me out of the corner of her eye. I smiled back playfully, but I got the message.

In April 1966, I met my future husband, Mwangi Mathai. He was a good man, quite religious and very handsome. He had also studied in the United States before entering politics in Kenya. He was also a very good businessman, and he introduced me to the business world. When I told my family, they could not wait to celebrate.

My first year back in Kenya was a busy one. As well as starting a new job and finding a future husband, I needed to help my family. I brought my two sisters, Beatrice and Monica, to Nairobi. They needed to learn to type to get a job, and I found places for them at a secretarial college. They also needed a place to stay and some work, so I rented a small corner shop. We sold milk, soft drinks, vegetables, snacks and other things.

In their free time from college, they worked in the shop and lived in the rooms at the back.

I did not have much money to put into the business (why did I buy that car?), but I did my best. I woke early every morning to buy vegetables for the shop from the city's largest food market. Then I changed into my professional clothes and went to the university. Beatrice did very well at college and found a good job in a government office. Monica loved the business and became the shop manager.

♦

Early in 1967, my professor asked me to spend some time in Germany, at the University of Giessen. There were things I could learn there that I could not learn in Kenya, so I agreed. Before I went, I asked Mwangi to help my sisters with the shop and to look after my car. While I was away, Mwangi sold my car to put more money into the shop. He created a company and bought the building. Eventually it became an enormous operation.

I stayed in Germany for a year and a half. I missed my family, friends and Mwangi, but I knew it was only for a short time. I was twenty-seven and gave all my attention to my PhD studies. I was looking forward to getting married, but I was not in a hurry. Mwangi felt differently and wrote often, asking me to return to Kenya. He wanted us to start a family.

I returned to Nairobi in the spring of 1969, and in May Mwangi got his wish. We had two weddings – the first was a traditional Kikuyu wedding at my father's farm in Nakuru, and the second was a Catholic service in Nairobi. I wore a long white Western-style dress and carried white flowers. I also had nine strings around my neck, one string for each of the married daughters of Gikuyu and Mumbi, the parents of the Kikuyu people.

Mwangi had decided that he wanted to become a member

of parliament, so in that year's election, I found myself in the middle of a political campaign as well as teaching at the university. Although I was also expecting a baby, I often worked all night for my husband's campaign.

I had to be careful. My husband might lose votes because his wife was a highly educated woman. Many people still did not believe in education for women, and some thought I was 'a white woman in a black skin'. We had many visitors to our home, including political enemies, but I received them all warmly like 'a good African woman'. I served them personally with food, whatever the time of day or night. I then sat and talked with my guests. My training during that campaign has stayed with me. If you visit my home today, I still rush to the kitchen to make you something to eat.

As a politician's wife, I was often in public. Over the next few years, I changed my way of dressing. I did not want to see embarrassing pictures of myself in the newspapers in tight dresses or short skirts. I began to wear long dresses, and I put my short dresses, trousers and high heels at the back of the clothes cupboard.

One afternoon during the campaign, Mwangi came home with bad news. Tom Mboya, a government minister and a member of the Luo tribe, had been murdered. People said the killer was a Kikuyu. This caused trouble between Luos and Kikuyus. It also caused trouble for democracy in Kenya. President Kenyatta took the opportunity to make other political parties illegal. For the next twenty-three years, there was only one political party in Kenya – Kenyatta's party.

Mwangi lost the election, and immediately began planning his campaign for the next one in five years' time. We had good news too, though. Our first child, a boy, was born at Nairobi Hospital. We named him Waweru after Mwangi's father – a Kikuyu tradition – and I took a few weeks off work before returning full time to the university. I loved those early years with Waweru, and then with our other two children, Wanjira, a daughter, and Muta, a second son.

In 1971, I completed my PhD at the University of Nairobi. I was the first woman in East and Central Africa to receive a PhD, but it was not reported in the newspapers. I just continued with my teaching and studying, and tried to communicate my knowledge to my students.

♦

My university work took me out into the countryside because I was studying a disease in cows. This disease was carried by insects and it killed cows that had been brought into Kenya from abroad. Strangely, it did not affect native cows. I needed to collect some of these insects to examine at the university.

While I was working, I realised that the countryside had changed from my childhood. When it rained, the rainwater used to run into the rivers and disappear into the earth. Now it ran fast down the hillsides and along the paths and roads, and the water was muddy.

'The rain is washing the earth away,' I thought to myself. 'We must do something about that.'

Then there were the cows themselves. They used to be fat and healthy. Now they were so thin that you could see their bones. There was very little grass for them, and during the dry season the grass was of poor quality.

The people looked thin and poor too, and very little was growing in their fields. The earth had lost its richness.

I went to visit my family in Nyeri, and I saw more changes. In place of native forest trees, there were large areas of non-native trees. But the non-native trees did not hold the rainwater, so it ran down into the rivers, taking the earth with it. The rivers were full of mud, and clean drinking water was hard to find. When I was growing up, native trees, plants and grasses covered large areas of land around the village. Now there were fields of tea and coffee everywhere.

I went to visit my favourite fig tree beside the little stream. A new owner had bought the land. He had cut down the fig to make room for tea plants. Without the roots of the fig to carry the water, the stream was dry. I felt deeply sad for the tree and for the Kikuyu traditions; mothers had told their daughters never to cut firewood from the fig. Even more sadly, tea plants could not grow there, and the ground was empty.

◆

As a university teacher, I was often invited to join other organisations. One was the National Council of Women of Kenya (NCWK). This brought together large and small women's groups from all over the country, and it was run by women who were successful in their business, professional or religious lives.

At one NCWK meeting, my eyes were opened wider to Kenya's problems. A group had found that children in the central area of Kenya were not getting enough to eat. This was surprising because the central area had some of the best land. But times had changed. Many farmers were growing tea and coffee to sell on the international market on land that local people had, in the past, used to grow their own food.

Because landowners had cut down many trees, it was also harder to find firewood. Women were having to buy white bread and white rice to feed their families. These new foods needed less cooking, so they were more practical, but they didn't have as much goodness as traditional foods. Children and old people were suffering the most. These facts worried me. When I was a child, there was plenty of good, healthy food. There was always enough firewood to cook with. But then the British had cleared the native forests and planted non-native trees in their place, so that they could sell the wood. After independence, Kenyan farmers cleared even more natural forests, so they could grow coffee and tea. For the first time, I understood the real cost of these activities.

Women in the countryside needed our help. How could they find clean water and firewood? How could they feed their children and buy clothes for them? How could they feed their animals? These were our mothers and sisters. These were our problems too. And the root cause of these problems was the state of the environment.

I have always been interested in finding answers. I thought about the situation, and the solution just came to me: 'Why not plant trees?' Trees were the answer. People could use them for firewood, for fencing for animals, to protect them from the hot sun, and to protect the earth. They could pick and eat the fruit. And the trees would bring back birds and small animals, and help the land back to health.

This is how the Green Belt Movement began. In 1977, I began a tree planting programme with the NCWK. On World Environment Day that year, hundreds of us marched from the centre of Nairobi to Kamukunji Park on the edge of the city. When we arrived, we were joined by Margaret Kenyatta, the daughter of the president, government ministers, local officials and a reporter from the *Daily Nation*, one of Kenya's main newspapers. We planted seven trees in the park and our celebration was on the front page of the newspaper. The seven trees were for seven heroes from Kenya's political history, each one from a different community. Among the trees were an African fig tree, an East African yellow wood and a nandi flame. These seven trees formed our first 'green belt'.

We tried to start Green Belt Movement programmes in

many places in Kenya, but none of these early programmes lasted for long. You need local people to believe in the idea and to give their time, and people did not support us yet. You also need to understand the local culture, and change your plans to suit each community. We had a lot to learn.

But news of the Green Belt Movement began to spread through the NCWK. By the end of the year, farmers, schools and churches wanted to start their own programmes. Communities were taking responsibility for their Green Belt Movement programme, and we have worked this way since then.

I was still working at the university, bringing up my children and looking after our home, but luckily I had a lot of energy. I wrote to many organisations and companies to ask for money to support the tree-planting campaign.

As the programme became more popular, the demand for seedlings grew. I visited the government's chief forester, and told him our plans. We were thinking big – we wanted to plant a tree for every person in Kenya. The population of Kenya then was fifteen million. We called our programme, 'One person, one tree'.

'You can have all the seedlings you want,' said the chief forester, laughing. 'And you can have them free.' He clearly did not think we would take all his seedlings. But a few months later, that's exactly what happened.

'You'll have to pay for them,' he told me, when I asked for more. 'You're taking too many seedlings from the foresters.' Then it was my turn to laugh. We could not pay for the trees, but we still needed them. So we had to grow our own.

We organised meetings with foresters and local women. The foresters did not understand why I was teaching poor, uneducated women to plant trees.

'You need a professional,' they told me. 'You need people with degrees to plant trees.' I did not agree. 'Professionals make everything complicated,' I thought. 'Anybody can dig a hole, put a tree in it and look after it.' And most of the women were farmers, so they knew all about growing things.

'Put the seeds in the ground,' I said to them. 'If they're good, they'll grow. If they're bad, they won't grow. Simple.'

That's exactly what they did. The women started showing each other, and soon they were growing seedlings all over Kenya. These women were our 'foresters without degrees'. They collected seeds in the forests and fields, and began to grow different types of native tree. We decided to give the women a small amount of money for each tree. It was not much, but it helped them.

We taught communities to plant seedlings in lines of a thousand to form green belts. The belts held the earth in place when it rained. They acted as windbreaks and gave protection from the sun, and they looked beautiful.

I loved to work with my hands. In the 1980s, some politicians made fun of me, a highly-educated professor working on my knees next to the country women, but I had no problem with it and the country women were happy to accept me. I was a child of the same land. The future of the earth is important to all of us, and we must do all we can to protect it.

Chapter 5   A Cruel Punishment

Mwangi had campaigned for parliament in the 1974 election, and this time he had won. Now we both had difficult jobs – he in parliament, and me at the university – and we had our young family to look after. There were many demands on our

I loved to work with my hands.

time, and it was not good for our marriage.

I was also trying to succeed in a man's world, and that did not help. Traditional Kenyan society values boys more highly than girls. Boys are expected to do better in education than girls. It was an unspoken problem that I, not my husband, had a PhD and taught in a university. Society's attitude shaped my husband's, and he had to prove that he was the boss in our marriage.

I realise now that the problems in our marriage began early. At first, for example, I did not take Mwangi's surname, but continued to use my own name. He thought this made him look foolish. Later, to keep the peace, I agreed to add his name to mine. But that was not enough. By the mid-1970s, our marriage was in trouble and there were difficult times ahead of us.

One day in July 1977, I came home from work and I knew something was different. Some of the paintings on the wall were missing, and the curtains, the record player and the television were gone.

A woman looked after the children for us while we were at work. She was there.

'What happened?' I asked her.

'Your husband packed all his things in the car and left,' she said.

I could not believe it. This was real. Mwangi had left me. I sat down and thought about our lives together: our wedding, the births of our children, the laughter, the tears and now ... this!

A voice inside me called out, 'Sweep!' I obeyed the voice, and started to sweep Mwangi's rubbish out of my house. As I swept, I remembered a friend's words: 'Life is a journey and a fight,' she had said. 'We cannot control it, but we can make the best out of any situation.' Now I really was in a situation. I had to make the best of it.

The following day, I woke up with a terrible feeling of sadness. But outside, life continued as normal. People were going to work as usual. 'Don't you realise?' I wanted to call out. 'My husband has left me. Stop, and cry with me!' But nobody knew or cared.

Luckily, I was a very independent person. I was used to making my own decisions, at the university and at home. In fact, very little changed in our daily lives. Work stayed the same. I came home and cooked for the children, helped them with their homework and put them to bed. And I had the Green Belt Movement. My marriage had ended, but my life had not.

The children and I moved to a new university house to make a fresh start. It had a large garden with several trees. The children were happy there. They enjoyed climbing the trees and eating fruit straight from the branches.

♦

Two years later, I found myself in the divorce court. I wanted to keep our business private, but Mwangi chose to divorce in public. The experience was horrible. Mwangi told the court that I had a lover. He said I made him ill and was cruel. They were lies, of course, and I denied the charges.

The court case lasted for three weeks, but it felt like years. Every detail appeared in the press the following day. It was a cruel punishment. And what was the crime? According to the press, Mwangi said in court that I was 'too educated, too strong, too successful and too hard to control'. The newspapers decided that our problems were all my fault, and they used my case as a stick to beat educated women. 'Look what happens when a woman thinks she is clever and can question a man,' they said.

I tried to hold my head high, and to suffer quietly. I wanted Kenyan women and girls to feel proud of me.

The judge supported Mwangi and I lost. I was now divorced and I was very upset. Soon after that, I received a letter from Mwangi's legal team. They told me that I must stop using Mwangi's surname, which was 'Mathai'. I was insulted and deeply hurt. I decided to add another 'a', and so I became 'Maathai' – Wangari Muta Maathai. I was still connected to my husband, but I was my own person.

A week or two after the divorce, I gave an interview to *Viva* magazine. I criticised the judge in my divorce case, saying that Mwangi had told lies. I said the judge was either stupid or dishonest. I could not believe the effect this interview had.

The judge was very angry, and I was brought back to court on new charges. I was given six months in prison. The police arrested me immediately and took me to Lang'ata Women's Prison in Nairobi, with no opportunity to see my children first. Now I had lost my husband and my freedom.

The prison was crowded, dirty and cold. At first, I was held in a room with no roof and nowhere to sit down. It started to rain, and there was water everywhere. Later, I was moved to another room with four other women. I was given a uniform, a haircut and a blanket. The other women were very kind. We all slept close together to keep warm. That night I worried about my children. They were still young, and I could not spend six months away from them. And I had done nothing wrong!

Luckily I had good friends on the outside. My case was all over the newspapers the next day. After three days in prison, my legal team apologised to the court for me. The judge let me go.

My experience in prison was a turning point. I could see that people were jealous and that they enjoyed my troubles. The message to women was clear: 'If you don't behave like a good African woman, this is the treatment you will receive.'

This message did not destroy me – it gave me strength.

Money was a problem. My university pay was not enough to keep me and the children, and I did not want to take money from Mwangi. I had a bill from my legal team, but I did not have the money to pay it. Then a job offer arrived: six months in Zambia with the United Nations. I could not take the children, because I had to travel all over Africa. But if I did not take the job, we would be thrown out of our house into the streets. Who could look after the children for me? There was only one person.

I put the children in the car and drove to Mwangi's house. 'I'm leaving the children with you for a short time,' I said. 'I'm coming back soon.' I watched those little children walk into the compound, knowing that Mwangi would take good care of them. In the end, they stayed with him for several years. When they came back to me, in about 1985, I was very happy. But I am also very pleased that our children have a positive relationship with both their parents.

◆

When President Kenyatta died in office in 1978, aged 86, Daniel arap Moi became president without an election and immediately started to make his position stronger. President Moi was from the Kalenjin tribe and he felt that the Kikuyus had too much power in Kenya. At that time, the country was run by a small group of men – businessmen, politicians and ministers – who all knew each other well. These were not the conditions for good and fair government.

President Moi's government did not like the National Council for the Women of Kenya (NCWK) and it did not like me. So when I was elected chairperson of the NCWK, the government was not pleased. Terrible things were written about me in the newspapers. Some important women's groups left the NCWK when they learned of the government's views, and we lost most of our financial support. We decided to put our energy into the Green Belt Movement, which was becoming well-known and successful.

In 1982, I decided to put my name forward for parliament. Very few women had important positions in Kenyan society, and those women were only important because their husbands were important. This was a big decision for me. I had to give up my university job before I could campaign. I sent in my letter to the university on Thursday afternoon. The ruling party then invented a reason to stop me trying for parliament. The reason was completely illegal and I decided to take the fight to court. At the hearing on Friday morning, I lost, so I went to the university to ask for my job back. They refused. After sixteen years of service, my job had been given to someone else in a few hours. The university was controlled by the government, and they clearly did not want me anywhere near the place! A cloud was hanging over Kenya – a cloud that would not move for twenty years.

I did not just lose the court case and my job. I had to leave my university house immediately. I had no money and no health care. I was forty-one years old, and I was almost down to zero. Now I had to pick myself up.

Fortunately I had bought a small house when I was still married to Mwangi. I had paid for it myself and put my name on the papers. It was not in a high class part of town, but it was at the end of a quiet street, and it was a good place to live and work. I planted lots of trees in the garden, and it became the greenest house in the area. I loved that house because it saved my life, and I lived in it for nearly twenty-five years.

I had time now to think about the Green Belt Movement and how to make it grow. We needed plans and we needed to win the attention of the press. We needed money. I wrote to the United Nations in New York.

One afternoon, I was at the Green Belt office when a tall white man walked in. He was looking for me. His name was Wilhelm Elsrud, and he was director of the Norwegian Forestry Society.

'We want to find out more about the Green Belt Movement,' he explained. 'We want to work with you.' This was music to my ears!

'We'll need to employ someone,' I said. 'I need to work, so I don't know how much time I'll have.'

'As you don't have a job,' Wilhelm said, 'why don't you take the position?'

I accepted his offer. The rest, as they say, is history. I never looked for another job; the Green Belt Movement became my work and my life.

The first money came from the United Nations. I was able to pay myself, and to employ a handful of young women. They worked in Nairobi and visited groups out in the countryside. Thousands of women across the country were planting thousands of seedlings, and my simple idea back in the 1970s was becoming a reality.

But it is easy to plant a seedling. That seedling does not always grow into a tree. So we decided on a new rule: 'First plant the seedling. Look after the tree for six months. Then Green Belt will visit and check the tree. Then you will get your payment.' This is still the way the Green Belt Movement operates.

We wanted the women in the villages to keep records for Green Belt. Either the women could not read or write, or they had no time for this extra job, so we gave the work to their husbands or sons, who had few opportunities to earn extra money. Part of the job was to ask farmers, schools and others to plant trees, and only a young man would have the freedom to knock on strangers' doors. Most men had been through

'Plant trees and you will help yourselves.'

high school, so they could keep records in English and their local language.

Over the years, we discovered that many of these young men were dishonest. They gave false numbers of successful seedlings and kept the extra payments. They did not realise that our records showed exactly who had taken these payments. But if this dishonesty existed at village level, imagine the dishonesty at government level!

As well as planting trees, Green Belt wanted to plant ideas. We started to hold meetings in our tree planting communities. We asked women and men to talk about their problems. As they spoke, I wrote a list. Sometimes there were more than a hundred problems on the list. It was wonderful to see people speaking honestly and openly, in their own languages, about their lives. When I asked where the problems came from, they always blamed the government.

The government was continuing the practices of the British rulers. Public lands were sold to government friends. Non-native tree farms were planted in national forests. The money from these activities was going to a very small group of people, who helped the government stay in power.

I felt strongly that people had to fight back. 'It's your land,' I said at community meetings. 'You own it, but you are not taking care of it. The earth is washing away. Plant trees and you will help yourselves.'

During the 1980s, the Green Belt Movement grew into a much bigger organisation. I was working eighteen hours a day, and I had never been busier. We were known internationally, and we received more financial support from the USA and Finland. We began to work in other countries in Africa, which were suffering the same environmental problems as Kenya. After training, Green Belt groups started in Ethiopia, Tanzania, Uganda, Rwanda and Mozambique. Journalists became more

The goverment was not worried about Green Belt when it was just planting a few tree seedlings. But we were discussing wider subjects now …

interested, and I was often invited to speak at meetings about the environment.

Abroad, I received many prizes. At home, I was under attack. The government was not worried about Green Belt when it was just planting a few tree seedlings. But we were discussing wider subjects now, including the environment and women's rights, and politicians started to notice.

By the end of the 1980s, dishonesty was the culture among people in power. President Moi's government had no interest in the needs of the people and continued to take away our rights. If people spoke out too loudly against the government, they went to prison, where conditions were terrible. If people marched against the government, the police shot at them. Many political campaigners went to live abroad, while the government forced many others to leave. The government played different tribes against each other as a method of control. Judges and newspapers were told to support the government. Kenya had only one political party and it was in the iron hand of a 'strong man' president.

'This ruling party is going to be here for ever,' we said to each other. After the 1988 'elections', President Moi said that his party would rule for a hundred years.

I knew we could not live this way. It was only a matter of time before I would find myself fighting the government. And I was right. The trouble started in a park in central Nairobi.

Chapter 6 The Fight for Uhuru Park

I was working late in the office one evening in 1989 when a young man knocked on my door. I did not know him, but he had some news for me. He had learned that the government was planning to put an enormous building in Uhuru Park.

Uhuru Park is the heart of Nairobi – a big open green space in the centre of the crowded city. It has areas of grass, paths, a boating lake and groups of trees. Millions of people use it for sport, meetings, walks, or simply a breath of fresh air. By 1989, Nairobi was not the 'Green City in the Sun' of twenty years earlier. It was spreading over grassland and forest on all sides as it grew and grew. It needed its green heart.

The young man's father and uncles were close to the centre of government, and he had heard their conversation about the plans. Although they thought it was a terrible idea, they did not dare to question the government. The young man had read about me in the papers, and knew I was not afraid to speak.

I wrote to the minister for the environment, and we began to learn the details. The government planned to build the tallest building in Africa, with sixty floors. It would house the office of President Moi's political party, the *Kenya Times* newspaper (the voice of the ruling party), a trading centre, offices, shopping centres and parking space for two thousand cars. This *Times* building would cost about $200 million.

This was typical of building activity across Africa at the time. It offered nothing to the people of Nairobi; it was all about President Moi and his circle of friends.

We discussed the building plans at Green Belt. First, we simply wrote letters and asked for information. I wrote to the *Kenya Times*, sending copies to the president's office, local government officials, ministers and the newspapers. Nobody replied, but a small report appeared in the *Daily Nation*.

We discovered that two historic buildings were in the way of the new building. They would be pulled down. I wrote to the head of the National Museums of Kenya, the United Nations and the *Kenya Times* (again), with copies to the other newspapers. Many journalists were interested in this story, and they reported enthusiastically on my new campaign.

People around the country began to notice. Many Kenyans felt powerless against the government, and they were glad that someone was speaking for them.

I wrote to the foreign companies that were putting money into the *Times* building. Would Londoners like an enormous building in the middle of Hyde Park? How would New Yorkers feel about offices in Central Park? I wrote to the United Nations. 'There are millions of silent, unhappy Kenyans,' I explained. 'What has happened to fairness in our country? The government is supposed to protect us and lead us to a brighter tomorrow. Think of the weak, the poor, the lonely, the fearful, the uneducated and the silent. We must not look after the interests of only the powerful or the rich.'

The government did not reply to me personally, but through the newspapers. The minister for lands and housing told the *Daily Nation* that the building would make Kenyans proud. The minister for local government told the *Standard* that the new building would take only a small piece of Uhuru Park. He said there would be wonderful views of Nairobi from the top of the building. In other words, they had no good reason for building it there. I replied with an open letter to the people of Nairobi. 'Do not be afraid of saying what you think,' I said. 'You know you are right. Speak while you can. If the ministers refuse to listen, President Moi will. He says he cares about the environment. He says he cares for his people.'

The subject was discussed in parliament. Members of parliament attacked our campaign, the Green Belt Movement and me personally. 'Who is going to listen to a divorced woman?' they laughed. 'If she is so comfortable writing to foreigners, she should go and live abroad.'

Public discussion of the Uhuru Park plans increased. Some professional organisations were brave enough to argue against the plans. More important, the people themselves made their opinion clear. The more the government told them to be quiet, the more they shouted. Many letters appeared in the newspapers from people supporting our campaign.

I felt strongly that I was doing the right thing. I knew it would take time, but I stayed with it. It was hard when people said terrible things about me. It upset my children, and my family and friends. Some days as I walked along the street, I saw people cross to the other side when they noticed me. They did not want to stand in the street talking to me.

'Why are you putting yourself in this situation?' some friends asked. 'It's not your land.'

'Because after they have taken the public's land,' I said, 'they will come for your land and mine.'

This was the heart of the matter. The government was walking all over people's rights and forcing people out of their jobs. Ordinary people were afraid and powerless.

Plans for the new building continued. In November, workers started to break up the ground in the park. I tried to stop the building through the courts. I lost, but I was not surprised. Judges in Kenya were not independent. The good news was that the newspapers continued to report the story.

On 12 December, Independence Day, President Moi made a speech in Uhuru Park. He gave his support to the *Times* building, and he spoke about me. I had 'insects in my head', he said. If I was a woman 'in the African tradition', I would listen to men and be quiet. Why had the women of Kenya not spoken against me?

Soon after that, the government made a new law: all financial help from abroad for women's groups must go through the government. This made it difficult to find money for the Green Belt Movement in the following years. Other politicians called for the Green Belt to become illegal. It 'has done nothing that Kenyans can be proud of,' said one. Just before Christmas 1989, the Green Belt Movement was thrown out of its offices. We had been in an old, wooden building next to the Central Police Station. This building was actually owned by the government, but they had only just realised. We looked for new space, but nobody dared to give us room. There was only one place to go – my house. On moving day, the police came into our office and threw all our papers and books out of the windows.

I only had one child left at home at this time. Muta kept his bedroom and I kept mine. The rest of the house became general workspace. I felt bad for Muta, who was still a teenager. There was no place for him to bring his friends home. He understood the situation, but he probably did not enjoy sharing his house with eighty Green Belt employees!

We took the fight for Uhuru Park and freedom onto the international stage. I wrote to many contacts in Canada, the United States, Britain and West Germany, and asked for their support. Journalists from American and British newspapers reported on our campaign. For the first time, many environmentalists in Europe and North America were hearing African voices. They talked to their governments. 'Why spend so much money on a useless building in a poor country that has borrowed millions of dollars?' they asked.

There was a high fence around a part of Uhuru Park, where they planned to put the *Times* building. One day in February 1992, I woke up and learned that the fence was gone. It had been taken down at three o'clock in the morning. That day, a group of women were meeting at Kenya International Centre in downtown Nairobi. When I arrived, the women could not wait to tell me: the plans for the *Times* building were dead!

The government had changed its mind. It was not going to happen.

'Let's go to the park and dance,' I called to the women. 'We've won!'

I think there were two main reasons for our success. First, the journalists were wonderful. They showed that the government was using the country's money dishonestly. They also allowed ordinary Kenyans to speak through the pages of their newspapers. And second, international organisations realised how much democracy and the Kenyan people were suffering under President Moi's government. During the Cold War*, Western governments supported any African country that was against Communism. They either said nothing about undemocratic activities, or spoke in whispers behind closed doors. When the Berlin Wall fell in 1989 and the Cold War ended, Western governments finally began to criticise leaders like Daniel arap Moi.

So the *Times* building was stopped and I was not harmed. Ordinary Kenyans now felt more powerful, and from that time we moved forward with confidence and speed. This was the beginning of the end of Kenya as a one-party state. It was a long road back to democracy and freedom, with violence and fear on the way, but we had started the journey.

Chapter 7 Unbowed

The political climate in Kenya changed over the next ten years. It became more and more dangerous to speak against the government. People were arrested and put in prison

* Cold War: a political war, after the Second World War, between the Communist Soviet Union and democratic Western countries, mainly the United States

without charge. A fear of political violence was in the air. The government's attitude towards the Green Belt Movement and me became harder. I was now a political figure and I had to take care.

On 7 July 1990, a big open-air meeting in support of democracy was planned in Kamukunji Park, where the Green Belt Movement was born and we had planted our first seven trees. Although the government said the meeting was illegal, hundreds of thousands of people walked, drove or took the bus to the park. The meeting became violent when the police fired bullets into the crowd. Several people were killed and hundreds more were hurt in the street fighting that followed. This terrible day became known as Saba Saba ('7/7' in Kiswahili – the date of the meeting).

I decided to mark the Saba Saba deaths by planting a group of trees in Uhuru Park. Over the next few years, government supporters tried to destroy the trees. They attacked them with knives, or burned them to the ground. But the trees did not die. The rains came, the sun shone and suddenly the trees were covered in young green leaves. These trees, like Saba Saba, gave me hope.

By the end of 1991, President Moi had to listen to international and Kenyan calls for democracy. He was forced to fix a date for elections, and to allow more than one political party to exist in Kenya. The movement for real democracy had a long way to go, but this was a start.

About a month later, a large group of us met to discuss the future of the democracy campaign. We received a telephone message during the meeting: 'Moi wants to give power to the army.' This was a clever way to stop the election. The caller also said that the government planned to kill a number of people. One of them was me. Ten of us went immediately to the press centre and spoke to local and foreign journalists. If the president wanted a new government, we said, he should have the election as planned. Then we went home.

Soon after that, the police began to arrest us, one by one. I decided to lock myself inside my house. I had strong doors with big locks, and I thought I was safe. Two of my children were studying in the United States, and I had sent Muta, my youngest, to stay with his father. I was alone.

That evening, about ten officers arrived at my home. They climbed over the fence into my compound, surrounding the house.

'Open the door!' they shouted, but I refused. Four of them watched the house all night. The news spread, and by morning friends and journalists were outside. I talked to the journalists on the phone until the phone line was cut. The police stayed a second night, and I made them cups of tea. They did not really want to hurt me, and some of them supported the democracy movement.

On the third day, though, they lost patience and cut through my locks. My door was kicked in, and three officers appeared in my living room. They took me by the arms, and drove me to the police station.

The charges against me and other supporters of democracy were serious, and it was a terrible time. I was kept alone in a cold room. The floor was dirty and covered in water, and I had no blanket. The lights were left on twenty-four hours a day, so sleep was impossible. I was fifty-two years old, my knees ached terribly and I suffered from back pain. I thought I was going to die.

By the time of my court hearing two days later, I could not stand. Four officers had to carry me into the courtroom.

'What have you done to her?' people shouted when they saw me. 'You have killed her.'

None of the judges could act independently at that time, but my judge was as fair as possible. I had to report to the police regularly, but I was free to go. As I was carried out of the courtroom on my way to hospital, people held up messages that warmed my heart. 'Wangari, brave daughter of Kenya,' said one. 'You will never walk alone again,' said another.

The support was wonderful. Muta, still only nineteen, talked to many journalists about my case. The Green Belt Movement sent out an international message that we were in danger. Phone calls came from the United States, from Al Gore and Edward Kennedy. 'What are the charges against these people?' they demanded. 'These arrests,' they said, 'will damage the relationship between the United States and Kenya.' The government listened to that kind of language, and nearly a year later, dropped the charges against all ten of us.

I stayed in hospital for some weeks after my time in the police station, but my next campaign had already started before I left. Many young men were arrested at that time for political activity. Their crime was often simply to call for democracy. The mothers of some of these political prisoners had formed a group, and one of them came to visit me. It was not a crime to talk about democracy now, so there was no reason for the sons to be in prison.

When I could walk again, I arranged a meeting with the mothers at my house. The mothers' stories were very moving. I thought of my own sons and brothers – I would do anything for them. I suggested a plan.

Five mothers and I met in Uhuru Park and walked to the office of a government minister. We carried blankets with us. We went into his office and I translated for the women.

'We want you to free our sons,' they said.

'We're going to wait for them in Uhuru Park,' I said. 'We have our blankets with us. We won't eat until we see them.'

'Go home,' said the minister. 'We will look at each case and take action.'

We went to the park. We knew of fifty-two sons in prison. We made a circle of lights, one for each son. People stopped to look at the dancing lights, and came to ask about our campaign. By the time it was dark, our camp had grown to more than fifty women. We built a fire to keep ourselves warm and sang freedom songs.

Two days passed. On Sunday we held a church service in the park. We put up a big sign, saying 'Freedom Corner'. Many men came to talk to us. Some had been in prison themselves and had suffered terrible treatment there.

'You see Nyayo House over there,' they told us, and pointed to a government building across the road from the park. 'Underneath that building are rooms where terrible things are done to prisoners. Many have died after their treatment there.'

We listened as the men told us their experiences. Many of us could not believe our ears.

'These things happened to me ten years ago,' said one man. 'But I have never spoken about them before.'

By Monday, our numbers had grown to several hundred. The sons did not appear, but the police did. At three in the afternoon, they ran into the camp, hitting people with sticks. Some of the young men in our camp fought back. The sound of gunshots filled the air. I was with some of the mothers in a tent. We sang and joined arms, believing that the police would not attack us.

I was worrying that our lamps would start a fire in the tent, but then I was hit hard with a stick. I was rushed to hospital with two other women.

I learned afterwards that the women in the tent did not run. They very bravely took off their clothes and showed the police officers the chests that had fed their sons. A powerful African tradition surrounds the relationship between an older woman and a younger man. The message from the women was: 'Is this how you behave towards your own mother? You should be ashamed!'

That evening, the police forced the women to leave. The government told them to stay out of Nairobi. A fence was built around Freedom Corner. All our blankets and personal things disappeared, and were never seen again.

We had thought that even this government would not hurt old women. We were wrong. They cared nothing for tradition or fairness. They told us we were a danger to Kenya and its people.

The story did not end there. We were unbowed. The day after the police attack, many of the women returned to Freedom Corner. They found hundreds of soldiers with guns, so they went to a church near the park, where some of them slept overnight. They expected to be there for one or two nights. They stayed for a year. They took turns to refuse to eat. As one woman became too weak, another stopped eating in her place.

When I could walk again, I went straight to the church. I helped to organise food and support during their long stay, and the church became my second home. Male relatives guarded the doors and protected the women, because there were many visitors.

One night in the church, we woke to find policemen outside, knocking on the doors. A government official was with them.

'Mothers,' he called to us, 'the president has heard your cry. Open the doors and go home, and your sons will follow you.'

Some of the women wanted to open the doors. The rest of us knew that the police would simply push in and arrest us. We realised that about five hundred soldiers were surrounding the church. They had been ordered to break down the doors. Luckily, many of them were religious and they refused.

The next day, the news was everywhere. The government was forced to discuss the situation with the head of the Anglican Church. The soldiers left the church and the mothers stayed. After that, our group of ordinary mothers became a centre for national discussion. Many members of the democracy movement came to visit the mothers, as well as leaders from all religions. People came to talk about their suffering under President Moi's government. People came from abroad. But the mothers were still in danger.

The government tried to break the group in a new way. They spoke to the mothers separately. 'We will free your son,' they said privately to each one, 'if you leave the church.' Four women accepted the offer and went to the State House for tea with the president. 'Go home,' they were told. 'Do not listen to Wangari Maathai. She is using you for her own purposes. We will free your sons.' The sons were not freed, and one of the women even returned to the church.

And then, suddenly, the government gave in. A year after we camped at Freedom Corner, the sons were freed. We held a service to thank God at the church, and then the women proudly walked out of the church with their sons at their sides.

◆

The fight for democracy continued, but the democracy movement was young and inexperienced. It did not speak with one voice. There were discussions, arguments and disagreements. Different parties formed, with different ideas. None of these smaller parties was strong enough to beat President Moi's party. All the party leaders agreed that they wanted to beat him, but they all wanted to be president themselves. We held meetings all over the country, and at least people were talking about problems in their communities and about the future of the country. Although I was very active in the democracy movement, I did not try for election myself.

There was a government campaign of violence against the new political parties, and at least two thousand people were killed. The elections were not free and fair. Together, the new democracy parties won more of the votes, but with 36%, President Moi's party was the largest party in parliament. So the 1992 elections were lost.

There was some good news. Six women were elected to parliament, and five of them were in the new democracy parties. Many more women won in local elections. Those women were very brave. It was hard to enter politics in a country where 'a good African woman' stayed at home.

President Moi knew that his government was in trouble. He turned to an old idea to strengthen his hold on power: tribal war. When independence had come in 1963, there had been an opportunity to buy land, and Kikuyus like my father were able to buy land from British farms. Many people believed that Kikuyus had taken too much land under President Kenyatta. Daniel arap Moi was a member of the Kalenjin tribe, so when he came to power, he used tribal politics to move some communities and give land to others. Violence between tribes followed, especially in the Rift Valley, where I had spent my early childhood.

Land is very important in Kenyan society. If someone takes your land, they become your enemy. It was easy for President Moi to start new trouble in the Rift Valley after the 1992 election.

People came from there, told me what was happening and asked for my help. Fortunately, I was in a position to take action. In February 1993, I invited several friends to visit the Rift Valley with me. Local guides showed us houses and schools that had been burned to the ground. We met families with nowhere to go, who were sleeping in churches. Many people had died. It was terrible, and it was done with the full knowledge of the government. We held meetings, often in local churches, and asked people not to fight back.

'You won't beat them, so don't try,' I said. 'Kenyan society is in danger if this fighting continues. The government will use the army to keep order. The soldiers will shoot their own people.'

We gave footballs to communities and told them to start football clubs for young men. 'When the ball is on the ground, they will forget their differences and play. Then you can talk to them about peace.' We gave seedlings to communities. 'When the seedlings are ready for planting,' I said, 'invite the other communities and give them seedlings. Tell them, "These are trees of peace. We don't want to fight. We want peace."'

The government was not happy with our activities, and stopped people from entering the areas of tribal violence. I tried to stay within the law, because I knew the government wanted to put me in prison again. I travelled secretly and at night. I covered my hair. I often left Nairobi in the early hours with my friend Dr Makanga. We changed cars every thirty or forty kilometres, arriving in the Rift Valley as the sun came up. We always took journalists with us, and they carried the news to Kenyans and the rest of the world.

On one occasion we were driving through the forest in the night when we saw a group of men ahead, carrying enormous knives and possibly guns. We stopped, leaving our lights full on. They crossed the road quickly, and we could see they were ready to kill. If they discovered us, they would kill us. I had never been so frightened. They only kept moving because they had no idea who was in the cars. We learned the next day that many people were killed that night in the town of Molo. Those young men had been on their way there.

The government received financial help from abroad, and needed good relationships to trade with other countries. So when international supporters heard about the Rift Valley, and came to see for themselves, it was good for us. I wrote to the president. 'I went to the Rift Valley to listen to the people,' I said. 'Please use the machinery of government to end the violence, not to make it worse.' In return, I received insults. One government official said that my plan was to destroy the government; I wanted to turn Kikuyus against Kalenjins; I was an environmental terrorist. Some women complained too. I was not following African tradition, one Christian group said. An African woman had a duty to obey.

These attacks on me and my friends were funny, but also frightening. The police arrived at the home of Dr Makanga one night, and took him away at gunpoint. At the same time, I began to fear for my life. Strange vehicles followed me in Nairobi. Was I going to have an 'accident'? I was afraid that the government would arrest me and then beat me, so I decided to hide. But before I disappeared, I sent out a letter to my friends around the world. 'The democracy movement is under attack,' I told them, 'and the government is causing tribal violence.'

I moved from one safe house to another, with the help of my Kenyan and foreign friends, members of the church and the democracy movement. During this time, I was invited to a big environmental meeting in Tokyo. I wrote and said I could not come because I was hiding and had no passport. I think President Moi was very surprised when he received a letter about me from President Mikhail Gorbachev. The Russian president asked the Kenyan president to help me get the correct documents. 'I am surprised by your letter,' replied President Moi. 'Of course Wangari Maathai is free to travel if she wishes.'

I left my safe house and got my passport, although it was too late for Tokyo. I travelled abroad – first to Edinburgh, then to

Chicago and Vienna. I spoke about the violence between tribes and the activities of the Kenyan government.

Although the violence slowly calmed, its effects are still there today. Tribal problems can be started at any time by politicians. The communities in Kenya are small nations. We are separate peoples, brought together by the British into one nation. But we have to accept our past, and look to the future. Then we can create a new idea of a nation, a new idea of Kenya.

Chapter 8 Saving the Trees

At the next elections in 1997, the voting was again not fair and the democracy parties again failed to stand together. President Moi's party was elected for another five years. I had tried and failed to get into parliament myself, beaten by government tricks and a traditional political culture. So I continued as head of the Green Belt Movement, and I was busier than ever.

During its years in power, President Moi's government had given large areas of forest or parkland to its supporters. Because of Green Belt activity, this was often done in secret. When a new building suddenly appeared on public land, we immediately wrote to the government. Often they told us that it was now private land. If the government continued to sell Kenya's forests, the Sahara Desert would continue to spread south. Life for millions of people would get harder as good land and wildlife disappeared.

In the summer of 1998, I learned that the government was giving away land in Karura Forest for private houses. Karura Forest is a natural windbreak to the north of Nairobi. This large native forest collects water for four important rivers, and is home to many rare flowers, birds, animals and trees, including mĩhũgũ trees. The Green Belt Movement had friends in Karura, and they told us what was happening. When I visited the forest in September, I discovered that men had already dug a road and holes for pipes. Work had not yet begun on the houses, but there were huts for the building workers.

We sent letters to the government, and as usual they did not reply. We told the newspapers, and the *Daily Nation* flew over the forest to take photographs from the air. Their pictures appeared on the front pages, showing how much of the forest was already destroyed.

In the first days of the campaign, we made several visits to Karura to plant trees in the destroyed areas. We always informed the government about these visits a day or two before. One day when we arrived, a group of young men was standing around the workers' huts. We went into the forest and began to plant our seedlings. Suddenly, the young men surrounded us, waving enormous knives. They pulled up all the seedlings. We were only saved because the building workers arrived. They calmed the young men down, allowing us to leave peacefully.

It would take more than a few knives to stop us. We returned several times, and planted many more trees. Then in October, instead of planting trees, we went straight to the workers' camp. We had twelve members of parliament with us and a group of journalists. Each of the workers had a long knife for cutting down trees. We asked them to stop but they refused to listen. They were ready to fight.

Suddenly, there was a lot of shouting and smoke. People were running in all directions. I tried to see what was burning. The workers' huts, lorries and equipment were all on fire. Luckily, nobody was hurt. I was sorry to see property destroyed, but why was it there? The workers all ran away and we left the forest. Nobody was taken to court because nobody knew who to charge.

On our next trip, we found a high fence around the building area and a large sign saying 'Private Property'. Police with guns stood at every entrance to the forest. We had to get in, because we had to look after our seedlings. On the north side of the forest was some very wet ground. They did not think we would try and get in that way. A local guide showed us the way. We all took off our shoes and stepped into the wet ground, including the journalists with us. At one point we had to walk across a fallen tree over a fast river, and unfortunately some of us fell in. But by the time the police realised that we were inside the forest, we were already watering the trees. People were surprised to see photographs of me coming *out* of the forest.

The fight for Karura Forest now became an international cause. The head of the United Nations Environment Programme described Karura Forest as very important to Nairobi, but the government just increased the violence, allowing the new 'owners' of the land to bring in their own guards. These were unemployed men from central Nairobi, who were happy to use violence against us. They walked around in the forest in twos and threes away from the cameras. This was a different, more worrying situation, and we decided to stay outside the forest and to plant a tree at the gate.

On that visit, we brought important people with us to protect us from violence. There were six members of parliament, Green Belt members, journalists, a few people from international groups and other supporters. This time we found two hundred guards carrying knives and sticks. They surrounded our group.

'You can't get into the forest,' they said.

'We're not trying to get into the forest,' I said. 'We just want to plant a tree here.'

'You can't do that,' they said. 'This is private property.'

'This is public land,' I said, and started to plant my tree.

The men became angry and started to insult us.

'Who do you think you are, woman?' they shouted.

This was very hurtful. These men were young enough to be my sons. It was also frightening. Violence can start suddenly, like a piece of wood catching fire. And it did. We suddenly found ourselves under attack. Stones flew through the air, and I felt a sharp blow to my head. People were running away, but I was rooted to the ground. Dr Makanga and another friend

'We just want to plant a tree here.'

took my arms and helped me out of the forest. The men threw more stones, and attacked our cars with sticks. People were falling all around us, and there were many broken legs and arms that day. We made our way to the main road, climbing over fences to reach it, and then to the nearest police station.

The cut on my head was deep and blood was streaming down my neck. I was very angry, but angrier with the police than the young men. I reported the attack, and we offered to take the police to the scene so they could arrest the men, but the police did not move. They gave me a form to sign, so I put my finger in the blood on my neck and wrote a red 'X' on the form.

A doctor at Nairobi hospital later told me I was lucky to be alive.

A news report on television that evening explained the behaviour of the police. It showed a policeman talking to our young attackers at the gate of the forest *before* we arrived. The story went all over Kenya and around the world. Angry questions were asked by many countries, international organisations, Kenyan politicians and church leaders, and by the newspapers:

'Why is it necessary to destroy the forest?' 'Why did you beat these peaceful campaigners?' 'Why is it a crime to visit a public forest?' 'Why is it a crime to say what you think?'

'I can't understand why you are against this new housing,' replied President Moi. 'Much of Nairobi is built on forest land. Our city is marching forward into the future. What's wrong with that?'

The trouble became worse. Students joined in, and some were badly beaten by the police. There was fighting all over the city. The students were angry about the forest and angry about the government's treatment of its people. For six hours they fought on the streets. The university was closed, and the president realised that he could not win the fight for Karura

Forest. One day in 1999, the president said that all public land would stay public land. All building in the forest stopped, and even our attackers moved out.

People tell me I am brave. I face violent men carrying knives with just a watering can. But that is not true. I simply do not understand why anyone would want to destroy our environment. Why would someone cut down the only forest left in Nairobi, and for expensive houses?

I think about the solution, not the problem. And when I have a solution, I do not see danger. We found ways to protect ourselves. When we were in a difficult situation, we often sang songs and danced. The angry faces of the men with guns then changed into softer, kinder faces. We were only women, singing and dancing. What harm could we do?

Today, the beautiful Karura Forest is still there, helping Nairobi breathe. The Green Belt Movement has planted more trees in place of the ones that were lost.

♦

In the late 1990s, my mother became ill and came to live with me. I took great pleasure in looking after her. Although she had probably worried about me, she had always supported me.

My mother had continued to work into her eighties. Over the years, her life in the country had become a little easier. Her house never had electricity, but running water arrived in the 1960s. She was part of the Green Belt Movement, and she grew tree seedlings on her land.

She was happy to come and live with me, but she missed her home in Ihithe. In her last years, we often drove there from Nairobi to take a look. She always believed she would get well and go home again to her farm. She died on 8 March 2000, International Women's Day.

I had already lost my father in 1978, and one brother and

some friends. When my mother died, I was more upset than I had ever been. I was not able to look at her picture or enter her room for a long time. I will never forget the many wonderful evenings we shared, sitting in her room and talking. My mother was not an environmentalist, but she knew the beauty of nature and how it made her feel.

When I was a child, my mother told me about the many rivers, wide and narrow, that ran through the forests on the western side of the Aberdare Mountains. The Gura River used to make a great noise as it rushed down the hills. Now she is gone and the rivers are gone. When I stand next to the Gura, I see only a little stream that does not rush any more. I speak to the memory of my mother. As my people say: *Arokoma kuuraga;* 'May my mother sleep where it rains.'

♦

At the beginning of the new century, we had great hope for democracy and the environment in Kenya. The international community abroad was tired of dishonest government in Africa, and elections were coming again in 2002. President Moi seemed to sense that the end of his time was near, and he planned to take an enormous area of forest for himself and his supporters.

Kenya's forested land had already fallen to 2% of the total. This is dangerously low for the country's health. The United Nations suggests 10% to make sure the rains come and food grows. By 2001, Kenya had suffered two years without rain, and many people had to be given food.

The Green Belt Movement continued to fight to save the forest. I was twice arrested again, and both times thrown into a dirty prison. But the government could not charge me with a crime, and they had to free me.

Elections were planned for 2002, and the democracy parties

finally forgot their differences. I decided to try for parliament again, and this time I felt I could win. The election campaign was not spoiled by violence, and for the first time in twenty-five years the elections were free and fair. Millions of Kenyans came out to vote. I won 98% of the votes in my area, so, yes, I became a member of parliament.

As the results came in, and a new democratic president was elected, tens of thousands of people celebrated, danced and sang in Uhuru Park. We had fought for this day for many years, and it had finally arrived. We had brought back democracy, and we had done it without fighting. And if people did not like us, they could vote us out. The Moi years had left Kenya in a terrible state and there was much work to do, but at last the future looked bright. I am one of the lucky ones. I lived to see a new beginning in my country. Others were not so lucky. But I have always believed that there is good to be found even in bad times.

♦

On the morning of 8 October 2004, I was travelling from Nairobi to my parliamentary area when my phone rang. It was a call from Oslo, in Norway.

'Is that Wangari Maathai?' asked a gentle voice. 'This is Ole Danbolt Mjos, chair of the Nobel Prize judges. We have decided to give the 2004 Nobel Peace Prize to you.'

Tears streamed down my face as I turned to the other passengers in the car. They smiled and laughed. What an extraordinary moment!

Journalists were already waiting for me at my hotel. My phone did not stop ringing. The hotel manager asked me how I would like to celebrate.

'The only way I know how to celebrate,' I answered. 'By planting a tree.'

'We have decided to give the 2004 Nobel Peace Prize to you.'

ACTIVITIES

Chapter 1

Before you read

1   Read the Introduction to this book. Complete these sentences.
    a   Wangari Maathai spent a very happy childhood in
        the Kenyan ....
    b   She had a good .... , which was unusual for Kenyan
        girls in the 1940s and 1950s.
    c   The Kennedy Airlift took Kenyans to American ....
    d   President Moi's government treated Maathai ....
    e   In 2002 she became a member of Kenya's ....
    f   Kenya did not exist as a nation until ....
    g   It became independent from .... in 1963.
    h   The Green Belt Movement has planted more than ....
        trees across Kenya since 1977.

2   Look at the Word List at the back of the book. Find words that
    you could use to discuss the following subjects:
    a   trees   c   politics
    b   crime   d   school and university

While you read

3   Circle the correct answers. (There may be more than one for
    each question.)
    a   Which of these did Maathai's family *not* have when she
        was a child?
        electricity   enough to eat   clean drinking water
    b   What did the 19th-century Europeans take to Africa?
        non-native animals   reading and writing   a new religion
    c   Which British cultural practices did some Kikuyus copy?
        drinking tea   eating with spoons   having several wives
    d   What did Indians bring to Kenya?
        trains   new foods   new diseases
    e   What happened after the British planted non-native trees?
        native wildlife died   some rivers went dry   forest fires

4 Which of these statements about Maathai's education are correct (✓)?

a Her father suggested that she should go to school. .....

b Her mother made the decision. .....

c She was six years old when she started school. .....

d She got very good marks. .....

e She learned about the natural world from local people. .....

f She grew too old for story-telling. .....

After you read

5 Discuss these questions with other students.

a How did the arrival of Europeans change Africa?

b Why was it important for Africans to keep their cultural practices alive?

c How does Maathai's childhood compare with yours? What is similar? What is different?

Chapter 2

Before you read

6 In this chapter, Maathai finds her mother, brother and cousin deep in conversation about her. What were they discussing, do you think?

While you read

7 Complete these rules for pupils at St Cecilia's. Use *must*, *mustn't* or *can*.

a You .... clean and tidy the school after breakfast.

b You .... eat snacks during the day.

c You .... sit and do nothing.

d Families .... only visit one day a month.

e You .... speak tribal languages at school.

f You .... do work for the community.

8 What led to the Mau Mau rebellion? Put these sentences in the correct order, 1–7.

a Africans had to start carrying a special document in their own country. .....

b Captain Lugard and Kikuyu chief Waiyaki
shook hands on an agreement. .....

c Kenyan soliders returned from the Second
World War with new fighting skills. .....

d Kenyans lost patience with the British and
started the Mau Mau rebellion. .....

e The British caught and killed Waiyaki. .....

f The British made African organisations
and newspapers illegal. .....

g The British took Kikuyu land. .....

After you read

9 Work with a partner. It is 1890. You are Captain Lugard
and Waiyaki. You are meeting for the first time. Have
a conversation.

10 Answer the questions.

a Why does Maathai think it was bad to make the pupils
speak English at all times?

b In what way are Kenyans still suffering from the Mau Mau
rebellion and the British response to it?

Chapter 3

Before you read

11 In this chapter, Maathai is going to the United States. It is the
1960s. What differences will she find between the towns and
cities of Kenya and the US? Make a list.

12 Imagine that you are going to study in a different country.
Choose one. What differences do you think you will find?

While you read

13 Which of these surprised Maathai when she arrived in the
United States (✓)?

a the tall buildings .....

b the lifts .....

c the white American accents .....

d the number of black Americans .....

e the colour of black Americans .....

    f   the racial discrimination   .....

  14 Which of these happened during Maathai's stay (✓)?

    a   Maathai felt very homesick.   .....

    b   John F. Kennedy was elected president of the
United States.   .....

    c   Maathai learned Western dancing.   .....

    d   John F. Kennedy was shot dead.   .....

    e   Kenya became an independent country.   .....

    f   Maathai was offered a job in Pittsburgh.   .....

After you read

  15 Answer the questions.

    a   Why was Maathai chosen for the Kennedy Airlift?

    b   How was the teaching different in the United States
from Kenya?

    c   What was Maathai's first experience of a 'green'
campaign?

    d   What did she learn from her time in the US?

Chapter 4

Before you read

  16 Maathai is returning home after five and a half years in
the United States. How do you think she feels about:

    a   seeing her family again?

    b   starting her first job at the University of Nairobi?

    c   returning to a free Kenya?

While you read

  17 Complete these sentences:

    a   When Wangari Maathai arrived to start her new job, ...
....

    b   A German professor offered her ....
....

    c   Her male students and colleagues didn't believe that ....
....

    d   She was the first woman in Kenya to ....
....

18 Complete this report to an NCWK meeting.

We have seen many signs of environmental (**a**) ..... .
The (**b**) ..... is washing the earth away. There isn't enough
(**c**) ..... for the cows to eat, so they are thin and unhealthy.
The people are (**d**) ..... too. Large areas of native (**e**) .....
have been replanted with non-native trees. The drinking water
in the rivers is (**f**) ..... . (**g**) ..... are hungry. Today farmers
grow (**h**) ..... and ..... where people used to grow their own
(**i**) ..... . Women are feeding their families with (**j**) ..... bread
and rice. There isn't enough (**k**) ..... for cooking and heating.

Chapter 5

Before you read

19 In what ways was Maathai's life going well at this point in her
story? Make a list.

While you read

20 In which order did things go wrong for Maathai? Number
these sentences 1–8.

  a He told the court lies about their marriage.   .....

  b Maathai criticised the judge in a magazine
     interview.   .....

  c Maathai's husband left her.   .....

  d Mwangi chose to have a public divorce.   .....

  e The government did not allow her to campaign
     for election to parliament.   .....

  f She gave up her job at the university.   .....

  g She had to take her children to live with Mwangi.   .....

  h The judge sent her to prison.   .....

After you read

21 Talk to other students. What do you think?

  a As well as planting trees, what other activities did the
    GBM organise? Why?

  b Strong leaders like President Moi are often bad leaders.
    Why?

Chapter 6

Before you read

22 This chapter is called 'The Fight for Uhuru Park'. What will the fight be about, do you think? Who will it be between?

While you read

23 Write notes in answer to these questions.

    a Where is Uhuru Park? ....

    b What did the government plan to build there? ....
        ....

    c Why were a lot of people unhappy about the plans? ....
        ....

    d Where did the GBM's offices have to move to? ....
        ....

    e Why was the success in Uhuru Park a political turning-point? ....

After you read

24 Discuss these questions. What do you think?

    a Why did President Moi want to build the *Times* building?

    b Was the government expecting a big campaign against the building?

    c What changed the government's mind about building it?

Chapter 7

Before you read

25 This book is called *Unbowed*.

    a Why do you think Maathai chose this title?

    b What do you think is going to happen next in her story?

While you read

26 Find the correct ending to each sentence.

1	People died	..... months later.
2	Maathai was arrested	..... after a year.
3	Charges were dropped	..... to hospital.
4	Women campaigned for their sons	..... to a church.
5	Maathai was hit and had to go	..... on Saba Saba.
6	The women had moved from the park	..... at home.

7 The young men were freed ..... in Uhuru Park.

27 Which of these sentences are true (✓)?

    a Daniel arap Moi became president again. .....

    b The government was responsible for new tribal violence in the Rift Valley. .....

    c Maathai and her friends tried to bring peace with footballs and seedlings. .....

    d Maathai became an environmental terrorist. .....

    e President Gorbachev of Russia gave Maathai a passport. .....

After you read

28 Discuss whether you think Wangari Maathai was brave. Which of her activities would you do? Which would you not do?

Chapter 8

Before you read

29 What is your favourite type of tree? Why do you like it? Tell another student about it.

While you read

30 Complete these notes.

Campaign to stop building in Karura Forest

Why?

....

....

How?

....

....

Successes:

....

....

After you read

31 Talk to other students.

   a What successes did Maathai and her country have in the new century?

   b Has *Unbowed* changed your views about the environment?

Writing

32 A property company plans to cut down an old wood in your area and build twenty new homes. Write to your local newspaper. Do you support or dislike the plans? Give your reasons.

33 You belong to a book club. You have just read *Unbowed* and you are going to present the book to your group. Write notes to help you talk about it. Say why you liked/didn't like the book.

34 Choose one of the photographs in the book. Imagine that it is part of a news report about Maathai and Kenya. Write the words to go with the photograph.

35 Write a plan for a tree-planting programme in your area. Decide on the number of trees, the types, and where to plant them. Say how you will protect them against the weather and wildlife.

36 Prepare a short talk about discrimination in your country. What kind of discrimination exists? How bad is it? What does the law say? Is discrimination getting better or worse?

37 Imagine that you are one of Wangari Maathai's children. Write a description of life with a campaigning mother.

38 Write a short report for an environmental magazine. Your title is: 'The biggest problem facing the environment today'.

39 The Green Belt Movement organises tourist visits to Kenya. Visitors are shown the beautiful countryside, and are taken to Green Belt programmes. Write an advertisement for GBM tourist visits. You can find more information at www. greenbeltmovement.org.

40 Find out about one of these other Nobel Peace Prize winners: Barack Obama, Aung San Suu Kyi, Amnesty International, Martin Luther King, Jr. Write a short report explaining why that person or organisation won the prize.

41 Write an imaginary conversation between one of these pairs of people:
- young Wangari Maathai and her mother, before Maathai started her journey to St. Cecilia's
- Mwangi and Maathai, after she returned from Germany
- Daniel arap Moi and Wangari Maathai, about Karura Forest

WORD LIST

arrest (n/v) the act of taking someone to a police station when it is thought that he or she has done something illegal

biology (n) the scientific study of living things

campaign (n/v) a planned number of activities that in time lead, you hope, to a business, political or social success

case (n) a question or problem that is discussed in a law court

charge (n/v) an official statement by the police that someone may be guilty of a crime

community (n) a group of people who live in the same area, or who have the same interests, religion or race

compound (n) an area that contains a group of buildings, surrounded by a wall or fence

create (v) to make something exist that did not exist before

culture (n) the beliefs, lifestyle, art and customs that are shared by the people in a social group

degree (n) the successful completion of a course of study at university or college

democracy (n) a form of government in which everyone can vote to choose the members of that government

discriminate (v) to treat a person or group differently from another one in an unfair way

divorce (n/v) the legal ending of a marriage

educate (v) to teach someone – a child at school, college or university, or an adult who is given information or shown a better way to do something

elect (v) to choose someone for an official position by voting

environment (n) the air, water and land on Earth, which is affected by human activities

extraordinary (adj) very unusual or surprising

freedom (n) the state of being free and allowed to do what you want

leopard (n) a big cat that lives in Africa or South Asia and has a yellow coat with black spots

maize (n) a tall plant with large yellow seeds that are cooked and eaten as a vegetable